THE NEW LAWS

Extracted from:

Tomorrow's World Order
By
David Gomadza

ISBN: 9781693117497
Imprint: Independently published
Copyright@2019 David Gomadza

NEW LAWS.

Section I

Everyone has a right to life regardless of ethnicity, genetic heritage, social status, etc.

Section Ia

Life

i.   The first laws that can never be broken are in relation to life. Recognizing the importance of life should be the sole existence of everyone and every government and institutions.

ii.   There must never be anything that can override this first rule.

iii.   Everyone no matter what social standing or background has a right to life that must never be traded for anything else.

iv.   It is a crime to end a life deliberately or indirectly. Even the lives of your worst enemies are now protected by our laws.

v.   No one shall kill and ever do something that leads to the death of another person globally and this might extend to other planets as well. Life for life applies.

vi.   Ending a life recklessly is against our laws. If you negligently or without any empathy do something that ends in someone's death you will be putting your own life at risk.

vii.   No laws will and must never override this first law. No national security laws must override this law.

viii.   Everyone has a right to self-defense clause and is entitled to preserve life.

Section Ib

Quality of life.

i.   Everyone has the right to the best quality of life free from any interruptions, invasions, harassment, etc.

ii.   It is everyone's duty to provide the best life can offer and achieve the best quality of life.

iii.   We must ban anything that affects the quality of life. Our aim is to boost everyone's self-esteem to the highest levels through education and showing how it's done by removing everything lower quality of life. Noise, air and land pollution all to be dealt with. Living standards to be improved greatly.

iv.   Laws banning satisfying higher needs without achieving a certain level of basic needs. A crime for local authorities and other bodies to provide below standard services and infrastructure.

v.   Removal of any toxics to life in buildings etc. Banning of fossil fuels by a certain date to improve the air quality and removal of toxins from fumes. Hospitals and doctors to be of the highest quality and no mistakes or dirty tricks. Believe in quality rather than quantity.

vi.   Highest paid best value. Very strict rules and anything that conflicts with the right to life and quality of life to be banned. No chipping with radiation or other dangerous waves emitting devices. More search and technological advancement to improve standards and quality.

vii.   Less working hours but high pay or alternative income sources. More time enjoying life and networking or socialization. Better education and better practices in food consumption avoid anything that quickly induces aging and diseases.

viii. Better research and methods to prolong life and keep everyone young. Express-command to put an end to this through our laws and courts as a deterrent. Strict laws to kill [as orders of the court] on the spot those who violate these laws by deliberately induced aging and using hidden devices implanted in people's bodies to cause wrinkles and all kinds of unwanted.

ix. Ban protection still practiced in other countries that deliberately 'give' people viral watermarks as ways of identifying people under this protection e.g. pulled iris or some genetic mark etc. These people are making viruses and then test them on the population under the disguise of protection. All this lowers quality of life. Everything is viral-based and will only act to reduce lifespan and quality. It's broad light murder better murder them first through the courts. No place for barbaric evil ways. Very tough on these.

x. Drag to court if you can prove that they are tampering with your system and are loading you with watermarks that will result in death and or conflict with the first rule. Countries doing this as institutionalized and systematic probably with orders from the top we must act.

xi. Express-command to put an end to this through our laws and courts as a deterrent. Collective punishment by the whole world for nations who think are above the law.

xii. No one is above the law you all must obey our laws or if found guilty through the courts die at the hands of the assassin.

Section Ic

Right to Self-Defense.

i. This is part of the first rule; the right to life. Everyone shall have the right to self-defend themselves.

ii. No one shall trick others or manipulate them to deprive them of the right to self-defense.

iii. No one shall and must not do something that will sink others in situations where they are deprived of the right to self-defend. This could be creating a situation where one will be enslaved to someone unfairly, so they are helped as 'slaves' with no rights to defend themselves. A good example is when a government makes deals with the banks or other bodies to trap people in debt with the aim of holding them as ransom when they fail to settle say mortgages or loans. Where the government will buy the debt cheaply from the bank of all defaulters but also put all those who defaulted on 'death row' or under its wings or given evil protection where viruses are tested on them or where radiation is applied on them as they ended up chipped and as government property. A lot of factors will come into play. In some cases, it can be argued successfully if a nation made Weapons of Mass Destruction [WMDs] to defend itself or to deter invasion and this depends on the following factors as well that will be considered;

iv. The level of threat and if they too have WMDs. Imagine if the USA, Britain, France, Italy, NATO, UN, ICC, etc. are all ganging up on Iran simply because they have oil and have nationalized this oil and nothing to do with human rights and to make things worse these nations which I will call the cult have nukes themselves. In this case, it would be a lack of good judgment for Iran not to take any precautionary measures to self-defend itself. In this case, it would be reasonable for it to have some form of weaponry that will give them any chances of survival. They might justifiably admit that they have WMDs to deter invasion and attack as a self-defense mechanism. It would be illegal for any of the cult members to attack Iran when they also possess the WMDs themselves. It will be illegal to invade as they will be in the same place as Iran; possessing WMDs for whatever reason they might give.

v.   If Iran can prove that the reason for the invasion is to steal resources, then they would be defending what is rightfully theirs and the method used is in relation to the threat at hand. It's not like one country has a right and 'Responsibility to Protect' no. All they need to prove is the right to defend what is rightfully theirs matching the threat to the weapons. They can easily point to Article 5 of NATO and use that to show that it's all the cult attacking, and the invading country or countries are just the 'front-line of the army' with the backups at standby mood.

vi.   They can use precedents in their favor and point say to Iraq and prove that the cult did more harm than the Saddam they toppled and their main motive was to loot the oil and pay the debt and to cause sectoral and insurgents to destabilize the country so that there is no stable government that will, in turn, mean reduced oil prices. They killed more women and children than Saddam since the invasion and insurgency or sectoral violence has increased ever since.

vii.   Iran or any country that meets the criteria can effectively argue that these cults and the so-called world leaders are not able to have everyone's interest. They are selfish and the fact that they are NATO members indicates that whatever they decide is never for the benefit of anyone other than themselves. They can point to NATO's Article 8 that states that all the members activities must be for the benefit of NATO and no country will carry out activities that will conflict with the aims and goals of NATO and as such NATO is a regional organization called 'The North Atlantic Organization' and as such anyone outside that zone is not their interest. In such a line the USA or any other country has its own or NATO's interest and nothing to do with helping them.

viii. Can ban the UN and refuse its judgment as they have no jurisdiction on anyone as they are biased and serve the interests of their creators and investors the cult. Even more, they act only to act as spying planes [U2 Incident] for the cult trading information for money. Mind you they are funded by the very cult members who founded them who are declaring war on oil-rich nations who are their breadwinners. They can't have anyone's interest.

ix. They can go on further to argue that the UN, UNSC, etc. all are biased and have no remorse or feel empathy with the local women and children if they are the ones imposing sanctions that are killing women and children then surely, they have no interest in helping anyone. If they can kill women and children with sanctions after sanctions why would they be concerned or care for adult males being tortured by the government? This shows that they are just there to weaken Iran and other oil-rich nations on the condition that if they are allowed in, then invasion follows. Look at Iraq. Saddam let them in and the USA and the British using psychological mind games followed and caused the death of 500 000 women and children.

x. If they can't show empathy towards women and children through non-use of sanctions there is nothing of use, they can do to help. Claiming invasion on humanitarian grounds of rebels cannot stand and is highly flawed. A miscarriage of justice an act of

7

aggression. Why show no remorse to innocent women and children who are killed by your sanctions in the first place. What they do regarding these innocent people is the litmus test. Show kindness to these then we know you mean business. Neglect and kill these then whatever you claim to represent is void.

xi.   Instead, the UN, UNSC, etc. should be brought to justice for false Pretenses that they can stop wars and bring peace. They must be severely punished for tricking people and giving women and children a sense of false hope that they were dedicated to stopping the war when they can't. Most wars have happened even if they had been invited and found no WMDs. They failed to act to stop the war look at the Iraq war all they could say was that the war was illegal but did nothing even to delay the war to give women and children time to escape the invasion to neighboring countries. Their existence and their declaration that they can stop the war when they can't and the fact that they have no powers is a miscarriage of justice and have led to the deaths of innocent people for the past seventy years. They must be dragged to the courts and face punishment and every family member of anyone who died when they did nothing be compensated until they are out of business. It is the greatest crime to give people a false sense of security when you can't do anything. This is because they block 'potential help' as people then assume that they are going to stop the war only to find out last minute that they are part of the rugby team to deceive and trick the defenders of the opposition so that their striker can score easily a try.

xii.   Our laws will put an instant end to all UN, UNSC, etc. We believe their presence perpetuates global problems. They are there just for cosmetics purposes just like mannequins in a shop window and to create jobs where people do nothing but expect a check at the end of the month.

xiii. Individuals can use self-defense laws as well. In cases where governments or people in positions of trust betray them by violating their right to life and to an excellent quality of life say by being loaded with harmful watermarks in the name of protection, they can use this defense to evade death, etc.

Section Id

Factors supporting the above laws; the right to life, quality of life and self-defense.

i. Implementation of new laws to safeguard human life and boost self-esteem. It is illegal to carry out acts or give commands that will result in the needless death of women and children no matter their ethnicity, background, genetic heritage or social status be it perceived or imaginary.

ii. Every life of women and children be it from the developed or developing world matters. It is a criminal act to carry out attacks or give commands that will endanger the lives of women and children. There is express universal expectation that all leaders and those in command will act in such a way to avoid killing women and children. In the New World, TWO shall make it a MUST that as humans we will have situations that will require enforcing our new laws and these will involve taking military action. In such cases, every tactical method to be considered shall OUTRIGHT eliminating or posing any danger to the lives of women and children.

iii. The main issue is with the initial tagging at birth that is illegal and unjustified. So new laws banning secretive human chipping at birth without consent and waiting for court lifelines to expire so that they further abuse the victims.

In the long run, the following will argument the right to life.

iv. Banning of all-time limits regarding the law. New laws overriding all current practices especially regarding medical practices in developed countries where the problem has reached unacceptable levels.

v. A new 24-hour system supplemented by the advanced smart contracts that execute cases without the need for judges etc. unless if the matter is serious enough or can't be solved.

vi. Stripping off immunity and using decentralized systems to encourage abused people to send information to the blockchain to be kept permanent and automatic linking to the smart contract system that starts the proceedings fast. The benefit that their parties mainly people in positions of power have themselves become so corrupt that they have lost the plot and what is expected of them. Removing these removes the situation of further abuse and intimidation with the result that the victims might be scared to come forward. The smart contract system allows people to do this secretly in the safety of their homes with information sent to other people within the block to validate before the smart contract executes.

vii. Banning of the making of any digital or cyber or any future digital or other technology that will conflict with the first rules.

viii. Any cases of death of the head of the house where the police and the doctors and nurses then went to take over must be fully investigated in most cases it's murder as the fathers had been in accidents where they are then illegally tagged and hacked which is often the cause of death as remotely gadgets are used to tamper with the body functions. This is hacking and a hacker just like a computer hacker has the following main aims and goals.

ix. To cause malfunction by altering the otherwise functioning system.

x. A hacker's aim is to replace the system and reverse functions stopping some and doing all kinds of damage remotely through satellites, etc.

xi. Hacker's aim is to hold the person in ransom using the person's family or assets in the hard drive as ransom. In this case, threatening to take over the family who they groom and teach "how to live their way" matchmaking with people of interest to them or giving these as gifts to celebrities and other politicians for political gains like weakening the opposition by associating them with prostitutes or abuse that damages their political or social career.

xii. A hacker, in the end, expects drastic change that result in malfunction or death.

xiii. The fact that it is institutionalized with orders probably at the top is a cause for concern and as such we shall investigate suspicious cases where the implanted devices are the cause of death through hacking by people in power or their delegates. In some cases, they offer the victims to prominent people like celebrities in exchange for political donations, etc.

Laws to ban such practices and stiff penalties in cases where it can be proved that the institutions encouraged abuse and waited until the person is dead to start condemning the problem.

xiv. Laws banning hospitals to own or get involved in drug production like heroin for medical purposes. Research and development into alternative medicines.

xv. Banning and stiff penalties for doctors implanting and chipping people secretly without them knowing.

xvi. Advanced research and technology that detect implanted devices by making them behave erratically that they can be recorded and the proof to be used in courts.

xvii. Laws to allow such evidence and use of phones and apps to provide such a technology to the world globe.

xviii. Again, uploading to the blockchain that can't be tampered with permanent transactions that can be revisited at a future date.

Revoking doctor's licenses and starting court proceedings.

xix. If the system is institutionalized in that the doctor's act was part of what can be regarded as 'initiation' then a change of accountability to include the order givers as well as the priority with both being punished severely. Change in law to summon the order givers as well as now it's just looking at the person who has committed a crime with the order givers walking away. Other laws can be used to bring the heads and order givers to justice too. One must prove that the issue is systematic that any one of the workers could have followed the order with the same disastrous consequences and as such then the order giver is answerable. You just need to prove that even if another person had followed the same command, the issue would have been created.

xx.   Again, no immunity for anyone if there is the death of a person and a violation of the first rule. Some accidents if proved still might amount to killings through negligent acts or intentional. We will bring in other laws where we assess if this is done just to say indigenous people then we can check if it is through undue regard to lives simply because the person feels distance to them and show no remorse or empathy and if the same issue had been presented to those he relates himself with them could he have acted differently, then we will not hesitate to punish and get rid of such a person. We have a rule that complements that first rule we shall call this Article 1.

Article 1

xxi.   A killing of one shall be regarded as killing the whole. Abuse on one shall be treated as an abuse on all. The underlying principle behind this line of thinking is the fact that some crimes threaten the fabric on which society is founded on and all international laws. There are universal laws that fall under the Jus Cogens and as such any derogation from is not just prohibited but makes one regarded as an enemy of mankind. An enemy of mankind means a Hostis Humani Generis a person who threatens all humanity and as such acts of torture on one trigger Article 1 and such a crime is viewed as if the crime has been committed to all people on earth. It is everyone's duty to take things into their own hands as long as they can prove precedents before or prove that such an act was an attack on all humanity.

What actions will trigger Article 1

xxii.   Illegal hacking secretive or otherwise. Hacking conflicts with the first rules in that it reduces life and quality of life and anything that conflicts with the first two rules is punishable by death by the assassin.

xxiii.   Hacking makes it easy to enslave people arising into secretive modern-day slavery with the hacked often with no rights at all with the hacker abusing for personal gains, sexual or other gratification of seeing someone suffering.

xxiv.   Hacking violates all international laws as it restricts the right to family life, right to privacy. Right to life. Right to a free good quality life. The right to freedom of speech as the hacked is tortured not to speak or report the culprit. Hacking is used as a form of evil submission with the victim tortured until he or she obeys.

xxv.   The hacked is deprived of chances to bring the culprits to justice as he is often followed through GPS and people told lies about the victim to tarnish his or her name to destroy credibility and make him or her not trusted. And as such is not believed.

xxvi.   Violets patents and trademark laws with the hacker stealing information which he or she can later show to the victim to intimidate or further abuse the person or maybe claim joint ownership of works they were never involved with in the first place.

xxvii.   Most people who do this have evil blood. Their past point to a dark phase in history where they might have done something maybe outlawed today like slavery. They might have been at the forefront and then looked for advanced ways of doing the same thing but now hidden and out of sight without any chance of being caught. As such, they keep abusing. As such new laws to look at a period in history when the accused might have done something. These issues must be understood.

Laws regarding everyone and the lives of military men and women.

xxviii. It is everyone's right to have a career and reach old age. Every effort through laws is being and will be made to safeguard the lives of military personnel. It is not an implied right to die by joining the military. TWO has advocated for highly trained military assassins to solve the problems at hand. There won't be a reduction in the numbers straight away but more emphasis on turning these to be assassins. TWO's priority to force the world to move away from defensive economies that priorities the military in that our best boys and girls are sacrificed way too early so that the political career of these politicians goes smoothly. NO.

xxix. The lives of these men and women matters.

xxx. Taking oaths of enlistment does NOT mean giving up their lives easily. It does not mean making reckless decisions and commands to end their lives unjustly.

xxxi. It is a law that putting the lives of our boys and girls in danger is a criminal offense.

xxxii.   It is every leader's or commander's duty to safeguard the lives of these men and women by making the right decisions. Methods to be used to achieve political objectives Shall consider this law. Where these men and women can be called upon to serve as they promised care has to be taken and detailed assessment carried out before sending them to be killed. Alternative methods and ways must be considered. I swear by the assassin shall be our motto.

xxxiii.   A tool to assess and eliminate the risk to the lives of military personnel. The military shall be like any other profession where everyone expects a pension and to die in the old age. Other laws that augment these laws are already in place, for instance, banning the manufacturing and use of weapons that put a risk to the lives of military personnel. TWO has advocated profusely for networking and cooperation. The idea is to move away from defensive economies. We are all one and we can all resolve our problems if not there is always an assassin, not missiles.

xxxiv.   It shall be every leader's duty to eliminate the risk of death in assessing military interventions. Any reckless commands shall carry the death penalty. Express-command to put an end to this through our laws and courts as a deterrent. The life-for-life soul for soul shall apply. Leaders will think twice before making commands that threaten their lives and those of the people they love. TWO shall make everyone highly self-esteemed that protecting life shall be everyone's priority.

xxxv.   Banning outright of digital-viral or biological weapons manufacture and use especially if they threaten the lives of women and children.

xxxvi. It is a criminal offense to manufacture weapons of any kind be it biological, viral or the new so-called digital soldiers' weaponry. All plants and bases to close with immediate effect and any stockpiles destroyed safely.

xxxvii. Owning, making, leasing or granting of such permission is a criminal offense punishable by death by the assassin. Where it can be proved that such acts are carried out.

xxxviii. Express-command to put an end to this through our laws and courts as a deterrent. Any weapons that threaten human existence are outright banned. The lives of women and children regarding such weaponry. It is a criminal offense to make weaponry that will end up being used on women and children.

xxxix. Weaponry that can be secretly used on women and children must and are outright banned no matter whatever the perceived benefits might be. Anything that infringes on human rights. Anything that conflicts with the right to life no matter how good other benefits are banned. The manufacture and use of the digital weaponry to command the population as is currently in other developed world is banned and not just a criminal offense but an offense that has express-command of death by the assassins.

xl. Any laws and practices that conflict with the right to life are banned. Priority shall be given to the right to life. There are situations where there is a need to control and command people for the safety of e.g. the monarch or other important leaders in such situations it is still a breach of human rights and the right to life and such practices are not just outdated but out of touch and they conflict with the right to life.

xli. The serialization of the population through the so-called medical records is not just illegal but conflicts with the first law; right to life. To carry out such surveillance and monitoring they have to use a digital computer-based system to give everyone in their population an identifying number e.g. national insurance that is then linked to a GPS and then medical records and such a system require implanting of chips at birth without the knowledge of the parents or individual concerned that most they don't know that these devices are being used on them and that they emit radiation and increases risks of cancers and other diseases are being used on them. The secret so-called commands are in fact based on viral-mutations.

xlii. Any use of viral communications be it digital-remotely conflicts with the first rules the right to life. Any form of communication and control whatever the main use is, it threatens and conflicts with the right to life. It is a criminal offense punishable by death by the assassin to manufacture, authorize and use such communications and methods no matter what the intended use is whether to monitor or for behavioral-changing studies.

xliii. The idea is to respect life. Such practices are prone to abuse and in most cases, such methods are used to unfairly abuse and enslave people against their wills. Such practices are done at the national level with the culprits doing this knowing that they are evil-doing never be caught as they can torture and abuse remotely through satellites and other local transmitters like devices placed on traffic lights or used in conjunction with the internet.

xliv. The military can be used to track and trace. Express-command to put an end to this through our laws and courts as a deterrent as this is no better than slavery.

xlv. You must understand that TWO is putting laws that can't be overridden to justify any prohibited acts. To achieve a highly self-esteemed society that will see humanity progress to the needed stages does not come easy or cheap. The first stages cannot be overridden or ignored. Everyone MUST acknowledge the rights to life. Any act that overrides this is not only in breach but also a criminal offense and an act punishable by death by the assassin. No men or women will deliberately carry out knowingly or unknowingly acts that conflict with the right to life. Being a soldier as explained above is not an act of giving up that right even though now it seems so. I have placed new laws that means being a soldier is recognizing the right to personal life. These men and women will and MUST put their lives and their colleagues first. They will have powers to refuse or override commands that interfere with the right to their own life especially if there is another way. Hence turning all of them into assassins. Highly trained soldiers that target and therefore eliminates the needlessly killing for the sack of killing. Mind you they are like leaders too if they recklessly kill, they become liable to be dragged to court. They will have powers to challenge situations that result in the death of others needlessly. Express-command to put an end to this through our laws and courts as a deterrent.

xlvi. To achieve our dreams and goals self-termination in any way is illegal and a criminal offense unless in severe medical cases where life will mean unnecessary suffering. Education and more research into suicides shall be given priority. Is there a link between hacking and suicides and if so, the hackers shall be dragged to court? Express-command to put an end to this through our laws and courts as a deterrent.

xlvii. An assassin will be given immunity by the courts as he or she is exercising the order and duties of our courts. If it can be proved that the killed person is directly or indirectly involved in hacking that resulted in someone taking his life. Remember life for life; soul for soul. Most people who self-terminate were abused and or illegal unknowing hacked at birth. The abusers and the hackers to face the assassin.

xlviii. Banning of the so-called behavioral changes methods as these are the real problems to be tackled and above all simply because these interfere with the right to life. Monitoring and surveillance can only be achieved remotely and through radiation-emitting devices and as such conflicts with the right to life simply because a gadget that emits radiation conflict and interferes with the right to life. In short, the risks of death due to radiation effects outweighs any changes that scheme will ever achieve. Express-command to put an end to this through our laws and courts as a deterrent.

xlix. No one shall command anyone else if doing so interferes with the other person's right to life. Who gives anyone powers that interferes with the right to life? In the New World, no acts will be permitted that interferes with the right to life.

i. Banning of professions that encourage the breach of rights to life. Professions that rely on illegal hacking of the whole society and monitoring them using radiation emitting gadgets will be banned. The police, some doctors and nurses are at risk in this line of thinking. The first reason is simply that this is easily abused in that they can frame people with the hope of monitoring them at a later stage through a remotely operated gadget under disguised and undetected. Such acts interfere with a person's right to life. Implanting a radiation-emitting gadget interferes with that person's right to life.

Section Ie

Global Leader, National Sovereignty and National Leadership

i. Declaration that the globe is a single entity and or should be such. Whatever laws and principles all affect the whole globe nevertheless each individual state will have its own laws and rules but also these must be complementary to the global laws and not in conflict. To achieve networking and cooperation, the globe must act as one limiting difference but maintain state autonomy.

i. Tomorrow's World Order is the global leader but has an overseer role where it is a mandate for it to establish and provide a working platform for all other nations to network and cooperate for the advancement of mankind. Its initial primary role is to act as a catalyst to speed up the shift from defensive economies to networking and cooperative. It must write laws and implement these. Laws that will spearhead the move away from the defensive economies. A framework to put things in place so that mankind won't revert to the 'tried and trusted'. A framework for proactive decision making and adjustments as we enter a new era and a new road with so many unpredictable.

ii.   A framework to find the best course of action and to guide everyone.

iii. A framework to act as the facilitator.

iv.   A framework to act as the negotiator.

v.   A framework that will help to impose effective laws that are fundamental to the advancement of humanity to the next stage of development.

vi.   A framework that will see our laws be obeyed and respected globally and where there are violations to assess the punishment and implement it.

vii. We are to represent everyone as we are not biased and can treat everyone fairly.

viii. Sovereignty of all nations.

ix.   Our principle laws state that each nation is sovereign in the fundamental sense that it's up to each nation to control its destiny. We are against the current thinking that some sovereign nations must be under another sovereign nation or established bodies like the UN, etc. who have no sovereign powers.

x.   A sovereign nation;

xi.   "Sovereignty. ... Sovereignty is the power of a state to do everything necessary to govern itself, such as making, executing, and applying laws; imposing and collecting taxes; making self-defense decisions and peace, and forming treaties or engaging in commerce with the foreign nation."

[Legal dictionary].

xii. We believe the only way to empower every country is to empower it to be self-sufficient enough in every sense of the word and be as sovereign as can be. We believe in empowerment to a level never achieved before and this can only happen if each state recognizes this and affirms its stance and believes that this is the only way to riches and solving global problems. We are against hands outs to sovereign nations.

xiii. We are against imposing sanctions to control and manipulate others, etc. We believe each sovereign nation can control its destiny. All they need is the belief and self-conviction that they can do it and do it. Gone are the days where nations look to other nations for handouts or look to the IMF for loans, etc. You are sovereign and we have empowered everyone never to take any loans. Never to ask for handouts and never to be sanctioned. We banned all these. If you are sovereign all this is within your power. You have the power to print and mint your own money. It's a right we will give everyone. Exercise that right. Sovereign means sovereign and we mean that.

xiv. We will ban institutions that sink other nations into debt through biased loans that are just there to manipulate and control others. The IMF doesn't have rights or powers to print or mint money so why rely on them? Master the art of printing money and fighting hyperinflation. Our currency will help you with that.

xv. Our fundamental principle is the sheer acknowledgment that each nation has the power to control their destiny and defined how rich they can be and as such must never look for outside help but to be self-sufficient and as sovereign, as can be.

xvi. Leaders, Prime Ministers, Presidents, etc. have powers to rule and control the administrative and external affairs of their nations if their actions don't conflict with our laws.

xvii. This also means that we have stripped the right to declare wars or make weapons or kill women and children etc. Otherwise, these leaders still have the same powers to rule effectively and make sound decisions to boost economic growth and development. They have sole prerogatives if they don't breach our laws, and everything must be complementary. We will empower them to have powers to make peace treaties and work well with others. We are not banning differences for we shall never be equal per see but we shall strive to be equal for some years to come until we have found common ground. We are not banning fighting for competitiveness aims no. They can fight each other if no one dies and without using weapons if that means doing it the old cowboy way so be it.

xviii. Linked to the above point is the need to see national and global debt as part and parcel of the advancement and development of any nation and global. National debt is an inevitable part of development and economic growth and must not be feared.

xix. Our aim is to increase the national wealth of every nation on earth and make all nations developed. It's achievable, and this is the only way to grow and increase the wealth of a nation. We have seen all kinds of fiscal and economic planning for the past seventy years and it's not working. Our strategy is to give every nation on earth a five-year grace period where debt is not to be feared or even talked about.

NEW LAWS.

Section II

Five-year printing plan.

i. We strongly believe that to grow and develop is only through the printing of money. There are no other plans or tactics that can induce growth other than increasing gradually the supply of new money. Only new money can increase growth. We are against borrowing from other nations or institutions like the IMF. The fundamental law of state sovereignty is the only vehicle for development. For a five-year continuous growth plan; every state must gradually and systematically increase the supply of their new money without fears for hyperinflation or national debt. At the same time, no external loans or funds must be accepted unless it's interest-free or your own. No international interventions that use local currencies with time frames.

ii. The fundamental principle here is to cut off paying any interest rates by borrowing. Printing your own is free and instantly increase supply in a flash and the only people the state or government will owe, are its own people.

iii. Printing money means the government concerned owes its people money and when this happens the value of its people increases rapidly. What's best to print money easy and fast with interest-free, boosting the economy and above all increasing the value of your citizens exponentially?

iv. Like I said the national debt is part and parcel of growth and must not be feared or give people sleepless nights. We have everything under control.

v. It is a compulsory global plan for every sovereign

nation that has and must have powers to print and mint their own money. Our plan is that for five years every nation prints money and increases the value of its economy and people, regardless. It is a must. I will explain later how to deal with hyperinflation, but no one should be worried about this if you do it systematically and periodically as advised by our team hyperinflation will not be a problem

vi.   How to deal with debt. The current debt is difficult to solve because it might belong to external sources. We shall negotiate with everyone concerned and see if the global debt can all be written off mutually before we start afresh. We have methods to deal with this debt.

vii.   Treat global debt as a depreciating attribute of a nation rather than as an asset that increases in value. Our aim is to be realistic. We don't want situations like today where global debt has risen to $244 trillion and still growing when we know there is no way we are going to resolve this and pay it. So, we shall use the principle of depreciation to deal with national and global debt. Each debt must depreciate with time. We shall nominate depreciation percentages for the whole globe. Say for example debt shall depreciate by 30% the first year, then 20% the second year and then by 15%, 10% and the fifth year by 5%. Meaning if you have a national debt of $100 million the next year the debt will have fallen by 30% to $70 million and so on.

viii.   We are acknowledging that debt is part of the system and it will always be there no matter what we do. To grow and develop a nation to borrow money through printing new money only which is a cheap and freeway. The current system of borrowing from others is increasing global problems.

NEW LAWS.

Section III

Dealing with Debt.

i.   How to deal with the five-year printing plan vis-à-vis debt. Offset rule. The idea here is that when governments print new money, it owes its citizens the debt. When it spends on the people and economy it boosts growth. What it must do is to encourage lending ideally directly somehow or through banks. We will work on that later. It can do that through banks in the meantime. Increase loans and mortgages. If the people defaults which must be seen as well as part and parcel of the system as a side effect of increased money the government must act and not leave its citizens the ones whom they have increased value when they printed the money lose this value.

ii.   So, what does it do? It's a government's mandate and obligation or duty of care to its citizens to bail-out them. Government bailing-out citizens and not banks. We are against governments bailing-out banks. Why banks? When you have printed new money, you increase the value of your citizens. When they are failing to pay you step in and bail-them-out through new loans and or mortgages.

Offset rule.

iii.   Initially, the government owed its citizens and now the government will sort of have paid the debt by bailing-out citizens. So, this offset the previous 'I owe you' clause now they will be on an equal footing. So, any debt is to be written off by the government without victimizing its citizens. This is the true role and reason for the existence of any government to be indebted to its citizens forever.

iv.   After five years of printing money, all the national debt and global debt must be written off. We have seen this method of dealing with debt for the past seventy years since all these monetary institutions were created and honestly, it's not working, $244 trillion is a large number not to act. Our methods have intelligent thinking and a sure-fire way of solving this issue.

Debt Relief Orders.

v.   A very vital tool to clear the ever-growing national and global debt. We acknowledged that debt is inevitable and part and parcel of the need to grow. Without debt, no nation will experience growth because you need new money which you can only print and therefore, we are saying it's better to owe your citizens than externals. So, the current debt must be dealt with a Debt Relief Order. It is absurd to think that we can grow and service the debt or even pay it off. So, we want real growth and be realistic. In the five-year printing plan, we cannot increase external debt. The only increase will come from interest on debt.

vi.   But we also agreed to treat debt as depreciation. So, on top of writing it off yearly globally, that is if your debt is external as the case with many. We must negotiate debt relief orders globally. We are here to be very realistic. $244 trillion can never be paid off. A new system is to organize debt relief orders globally. See who owes who and negotiate to write it off and start again. After we have written off this debt, no nation shall owe others any debt. The only debt acceptable will be internal debt owed to citizens the only debt that will increase their value.

Dangers of external debt.

vii.   There is the idea of sovereign risk discussed above. External debt makes people indebted to others and increases the likelihood of being attacked by the lender. In most cases, the lender has more power than the recipient and that is the reason why the nation lends out in the first place. If you default, they can impose sanctions or hold the whole nation to ransom. Recall our laws gives everyone rights to life, to a good quality life and to self-defense. External debt conflicts with all these. The more you borrow the more you increase the chances of being attacked. If sanctions imposed this affects the quality of life as more women and children die for lack of basics. You can't self-preserve or defend yourself and above all, you lose your sovereignty. You can end up a puppet who can't print own money and therefore are not guaranteed rights to become wealth the easy and cheap way through printing new money.

Laws relating to people.

viii.   The current international laws apply but we have given these priorities and the highest rank in importance and all can't be overruled by any laws including national security laws. We have banned wars and weapons and leaders will have powers to laws for self-defense. It will be a crime to wage a war or provoke others aggressively or incite wars. We are not banning unarmed conflicts I think for the initial stages that should be part and parcel of the whole process until a time when we will say that's it. Our laws focus on people and believe that everything should follow from there.

Emphasis of protection from unlawful killings.

ix.   Even your enemies' civilians are protected by our laws. Any activities or rules that conflict with freedom to movement, speech, participate in the society, rights to freedom from torture, human degrading treatment, rights to privacy, family life, freedom of association, etc. are not to be breached or interfered with. At this stage we take these rights to be part of the basics even if we don't mention it here.

NEW LAWS.

Section IV

People come first; the rest will follow is our guiding principle.

i.   We emphasize rights to private property. This is a fundamental right that is paramount and a cornerstone to the success of our aims and goals. We are for the emancipation and empowerment of everyone. We believe rights to wealth must be a basic right. Everyone must own property and wealth. It is the duty of a government to make sure that it increases the wealth of its people through printing money.

ii.   Related to this point is the fact that It is the government's obligation and duty of care to preserve the wealth the citizens have acquired by offering loans and mortgages during the five-year printing plan. It is the government's responsibility to bail-out its citizens and not banks.

iii.   It is illegal for governments to favor monetary gains as opposed to the welfare of its people. It is a criminal offense to emphasize the balance sheet and not the welfare of your people. There is no point in a perfect balance sheet when living standards are mediocre or below the global standard. Our laws change the mindset of everyone. Start thinking about people. You re in power because of the people. Print money and boost wealth and use the offset rule to write off the debt after all you owe these people your citizens. Have a crooked unbalancing balance sheet and a happy wealthy nation.

iv.   It is illegal to have standards below what we deem as

33

minimal globally. So, our plan is to increase the wealth of every nation in five years drastically to levels never achieved before. After the five years we shall write off all debt and the current debt will have been written off or depreciated. A new start and a new equal or almost equal level for everyone. We shall declare what standards are minimum. After that falling below that standard will see your leaders punished.

v.   We shall have tough laws for negligence and a lack of the duty of care to the people who put you in power. The E-laws will haunt you. The aims of every government are to increase the nation's wealth and improve living standards. Austerity measures shall get you punished under our laws for willful negligent, lack of the duty of care and above all for lack of empathy towards your own citizens who are suffering. It is your duty as the one empowered to print money to make sure that minimum living standards are met.

NEW LAWS.

Section V

Rights to Wealthy.

i.   This is linked to the rights to the property above but wealth here is broader to include other than property, e.g. shares, stocks, and bonds. It is the government's duty of care to protect the wealth of its citizens by laws safeguarding them. It must be the mandate of the government to bail-out its citizens first and not wait for repossessions first before they can act. Any loans by the government to its citizens are to be treated as having a depreciation effect in that they reduce or lose value with time rather than gain with interests. Banks can do this but not the government. We shall establish a way where the government will lend in addition to banks and government to be not for profit but to provide a service.

ii.   The governments must not confiscate or seize their citizen's wealth unless obtained illegally. When the citizens are in debt, the government will negotiate to have the debt written off rather than have the wealth already accumulated seized. Again, debt must be treated as having a depreciation value. Laws to be changed or new ones to come into effect protecting the citizens. A certain percentage can be seized as not to encourage bad behavior on the part of the citizens and any unlawful dealing can make them punishable by our laws but care and priority to be given in wealth preservation than destroying it.

iii.   The government to view its role as to build its citizen's wealth and provide perpetual loans and mortgages.

NEW LAWS.

Section VI

Section VIa

Citizens' eligibility criteria.

i.   As not to encourage bad behavior a criterion must be met by the citizens in all aspects mentioned above. To get a loan a certain criterion must be considered. Our aim is to change the current situation to increase wealth to new never witnessed before levels and we can only do this if we change attitude and thinking. So sometimes even if people can't meet the criteria but are of a certain age and are willing to earn more money to service and pay the loans, they might be eligible. The government will then depreciate the loan over the years to help these people say, new homeowners, etc. That is why we are going to print free money for the next five years of the plan. In the end, write off all the debt at the same time boosting living standards to new high levels.

ii.   The government when printing money will print some that 'will act as depreciation' in that a certain percentage is regarded as irrecoverable and a certain account put aside to compensate for this loss. If out of $100 million printed say $20 million might not be recovered the government can or might print $120 million and set aside the $20 million in a default account to act as depreciation and the loans over the years will lose value with depreciation being deducted yearly helping the people be debt-free and be able to pay back the reminder with time.

iii.   You must understand that our aim is for growth and development and improving living standards to new levels and not with a perfect balance sheet.

NEW LAWS.

Section VII

Governments and institutions.

i.   I believe some governments within the Euro and globally might not have the right to print money. I think that is a lost opportunity and one that must be corrected. So, all governments like Portugal or Luxemburg must have printing powers to print their own currency we don't want people relying on others.

ii.   Buying or using other people's money is expensive and will mean you being in debt forever. We are against this. If you are sovereign, then take control of your destiny and print!

iii.   Any institutions with the sovereignty rights or powers to print money but rely on other countries like the US are to be banned. No offense or underestimate the hard work they have done. But they rely on debt and interest and to be honest they are run like businesses and to me loan sharks. Whatever they do is to make a kill and run or sink the people in debt to justify their existence. Or they will stifle progress and development to keep their jobs. Why if you are sovereign with powers to print money then go and get loans from institutions below you? Empowerment and education must play a crucial role here. Never take your privileges for granted use them.

iv.   I think it will be doing everyone justice to ban institutions like the IMF that are political in nature and do little to alleviate poverty, etc.

v.   My view is that they give nations a false sense of security that they can always get a loan. Loans are expensive and will sink you in debt if they are external and loans remove the value from your own citizens if they are external. The best way that is cheap and free and readily available without interest worries is by printing. It's like if you want to grow you eat more food that will make you grow all you have to do is increase intake.

vi.   To establish a framework that makes everything transparent and fair. Corruption is a real problem, especially when printing money. No point to print money to be stolen by a few people because the wealth of the whole citizens will not go up. It's not just a case of printing money. Establish transparency by using methods that can be checked by everyone. New technology like the blockchain needed to make sure that an audit can be done to make sure that citizens are receiving the loans and the distribution is national without having increased inequality as well. It's not a simple thing to do. A comprehensive approach is needed. To remove corrupt people and a system to remove government bureaucracy and waste. If these are not controlled, surely it will be pointless to print. This will worsen the issue. As the money can be siphoned abroad to swiss accounts etc. and not increasing the local wealth. Hyperinflation can rack havoc in such cases.

vii.   The NGOs, the UN, other institutions, etc. are all part of the 'rugby team' I mentioned above. Rugby team and what is its role?

viii.   The UN, NGOs, NATO, etc. are there just to:

ix.   To give a false sense of security so people don't panic until the last minute but then it will be too late.

x.   They are there to block others who might complain and veto or stop the invasion until the last minute provide the invading country with clear access and less resistance.

xi. There are there to help the invading nation and its Allies carry out a strategic SWOT analysis as part of the risk management in order to reduce casualties and make the invasion short and fast. They are like spy planes (see U2 1960 spy plane incident.)

xii. They are corn artist tricking people when they have no powers at all even when they have not discovered any weapons, they can't act at all. They have courts but their judgments are useless no one listens. So, what is the point? They are a risk weakening the to-be-invaded leaders testing their ability to withstand an invasion playing psychological games putting lives at risk.

xiii. Even after the war and deaths, they can't arrange compensation schemes, etc.

xiv. They help perpetuate the status quo of exploitation where the West uses weapons to go and take what they want when they run out of money to pay debt and Justify that on humanitarian grounds. Altogether they kill more innocent women and children within a short time than the dictator they are removing.

xv. They are the ones to impose sanctions that further or initially cause severe hardship and deaths.

xvi. They are the same as terrorists in that they use women and children for bargain reasons through sanctions just like the terrorists who kill women and children.

xvii. Even if they don't know it, they are part of the post-colonial movement to maintain colonial thinking where the alpha middle eastern males are targeted through military action by the superpowers while the UN through the ICC targets the least threats in the

African alpha males. To them, oil, means power, as it means money and opportunities for new technology.

xviii.   What is happening is that the West especially the superpowers sell the evil technology to the developed nations e.g. the US selling nuclear processing or enriching technology to Iran then later send the UN to investigate if the technology is used for nuclear weapons.

xix.   As such to ban all these institutions or drag to court. Let compensation claims sink them down.

NEW LAWS.

Section VIII

Section VIIIa

Our Stance on deaths by chemical weapons.

i.   We stand with the international community to strongly declare war on regimes that kill especially their own people through chemical weapons. Our laws are against any deaths whatever the situation. Everyone on earth including governments must recognize our first laws; the rights to life and to self-preserve. Any death by any means for us can bring the whole globe still. This is true as we believe that such an act can make a person regarded as an enemy of the people if they use chemical weapons that can kill many. Did the joint missile attacks result in the deaths of civilians? Luckily there were no reports of any civilian deaths as a result of the joint attacks something that is good even though we disagree with the invasion of a sovereign nation when your own track record is hanging by a thread. So why they did that? This can be best answered by President Trump's words according to a BBC report;

ii.   "The purpose of our actions tonight is to establish a strong deterrent against the production, spread and use of chemical weapons," he said. [BBC April 2018.]

Our laws regarding the above incident and any related future ones.

iii.   Implementation of laws vehemently prohibiting making, possession, and use of chemical weapons with the aim to kill others. We are not banning all chemical weapons only those used for killing, blinding or maiming others.

iv.   Everyone must acknowledge reading and

understanding our laws and confirming this at their own time within a given time frame. We shall have a ban that is universal. Any breach will have serious consequences. We shall expect every nation to act as responsible as they can and obey our laws.

v.   For the purpose of the right to self-preserve, we shall protect all nations and give them rights to deny the UN and its subsidiaries' rights of entry into sovereign territory simply because for the past seventy-years their entry had been followed by military action. They might be doing 'good' but overall, they jeopardize the lives of millions of women and children through sanctions that are aimed to weaken first and then through them encouraging wars.

vi.   Banning of any form of inspectors on the grounds who are being used to carry out a Colony Collapse Strategy where nations are targeted according to the resources they have and not simply because of their human rights abuses. Saddam in 25 years is reported to have killed 250 000 and the Iraq war in 13 years or less claimed the lives of 500 000. Therefore, we argue and believe that the Weapons Inspectors only help the West carry out a SWOT analysis that will lead to an invasion. A strategic military assessment of the effects of an invasion. If they had not entered, the war could not have happened that is our belief.

vii.   Honestly, the UN and all its subsidiaries if they have no power to stop any wars are a risk to the lives of women and children as they are part of the rugby's tactical team blocking any kind of help from people who have the power to stop the war.

viii.   It is a fact the UN is there just to create jobs and nothing to do with stopping wars. It never attempted to create laws that ban weapons. In this case; guns kill people without guns we have no gun deaths.

ix.   We strongly condemn wars because just like terrorists the West is using women and children as bargaining tools and see them just as collateral damage using sanctions to cause severe sufferings simply because these people have no one to defend them. Now a thing of the past.

x.   No nations must group to attack a weak nation. The idea is to provoke a strong nation like Russia or China to try to defend the weaker nation in Syria and the Allies in Britain, France, and the USA then attack it. Such an attack can be disguised and used to attack the vital defense system of any country as this affect their right to self-preserve. Our new laws are a shift from the current ideology where military action can be carried simply because of the suspected use of chemical weapons. It's easy now because no one must prove that the weapons were used before attacking. They just attack and apologize later, look at Iraq the fraudulent dossier and now the OPCW's report is and was a scam that the Syria planes dropped the chlorine cylinders. We can see a pattern developing.

xi.   We must encourage the affected nations to take legal action against the UN, where the UN and all its bodies have entered on false beliefs and intentions of carrying out inspection that resulted in military attacks. Wherever the UN had entered and compiled a report that suggested that there were no WMDs but then went on to fail to stop the war and protect the innocent lives of women and children that it exposed naked. These nations must bring criminal intent war crime charges against the UN and its subsidiary bodies. This is fair because such entry gave the Allies a strategic advantage they would not have had. I will rely on the development of digital soldiers or gadgets that can be implanted or worn to pass information through a satellite that can be used for military invasion purposes.

xii. Where ever there were deaths of innocent women and children the nation invaded by the UN and its subsidiary were allowed-in must claim compensation for every person who died as a result of direct military action and indirect as long as it can be proved that the war was responsible for the deaths. E.g. the bombing of a bridge that is used for medical supplies with the resultant deaths.

xiii. The nation invaded after the UN had entered on false grounds to carry out inspection but resulted in the invasion must claim compensation for damages to infrastructure and other psychological trauma.

xiv. There shall never be time frames or time limits and there shall never be limits of compensation.

xv. Any nation shall bring charges of spying and acts of aggression again the UN and all its subsidiaries as long as their entry resulted in an invasion in which as the so-called peacekeepers did nothing to stop the war even after declaring that there were no Weapons of Mass Destruction.

xvi. Acts of aggression.

xvii. Forced entry in this cause cannot be limited to unauthorized entry by the UN to inspect but can and must include instances like the Iraq and the Syrian incidents where sanctions by the same UN bodies have weakened the government concerned to such an extent that he would invite them not just to clear his name but on humanitarian grounds to lessen the impact and severity of these barbaric tactics to save the lives of women and children. The fact that the UN and other subsidiary bodies are the ones imposing sanctions in the first place even if the leader invites them, we must recognize that he did invite them only to save lives. It's a barbaric way disguised as a cooperation tool. Our laws will make this a criminal case if there are deaths related to sanctions. The leader of the invaded country only had to prove that he invited them to save lives in other words to self-defend the lives of his people and as such justified and supported by the law.

xviii. Acts of aggression shall not be limited to the obvious invasion but will include the use of sanctions as well. Such use is intended 'to force the way in' and use innocent people as bargaining tools. We see no difference in such tactics as those used by terrorists. The fact that one man's terrorist is another man's freedom fighter might apply here.

xix. Education in psychological thinking can benefit developing countries and laws shall make it mandatory that leaders through our teaching materials etc. must be equipped with all kinds of tricks which we will expose.

xx. False flagging is banned and must become a war crime if such an action resulted in the deaths of innocent people.

xxi. If the West the USA, Britain and France's missiles had killed even one civilian new war crimes would have been brought against them. We are serious about global peace and our laws will take these cowboys. We are not able to bring reckless endangerment of life for personal gain and regardless of the lives of innocent women and children simply because they don't relate to the victims. Make no mistake this is a lack of empathy that amounts to gross human abuse simply because the West does not sympathize with the victims simply because of different backgrounds. I think this was proven after the 9/11 attack where Bush chooses military action that killed as many in retaliation or not while Obama who has a Muslim background decide to send assassins to do the dirty work. If it was a non-muslin non-person of color President, he might have used military force to invade Pakistan to kill Osama. We want to assess the law from all angles and be as perfect as we can be.

xxii. Personal gains of any military action.

xxiii. We shall assess any personal gains resulting from military action. We shall assess the reasons forward as justifications for war. For instance, to topple a dictator and assess how many the dictator is alleged to have killed and how long that took and assess the military intervention and how many people they have killed and if there are personal gains, we assess these too. A good example is 9/11. Initially, the Whitehouse had $2,3 trillion missing. Assuming all this money was consumed through purchases of oil resources. Recall President Dwight Eisenhower arguments that oil depletes a nation's resources. We can say that the war was embarked to make oil production increased in volume thereby lowering the price of fuel and thereby saving the government money. We will need to assess the number who die as well say 500 000 and check if likely cost of such a loss by calculating compensation or life insurance policies. We can check the broader impact of such an act and use that to bring perpetrators to justice. On the other side we can check to see if just before the war the country concerned was in debt failing to pay debt and if they managed after the war if so then we can bring more war crimes that they killed such a number so that they can raise this money for such a debt and therefore evil and must be punished.

xxiv. The idea is not just to deter but to change the way these leaders view life. There is a new sheriff in town one might suggest.

xxv. We are not against the West, but we believe as the titles reflect the West is a group of developed nations. Nations that ideally must lead by example and guide the developing nations. These nations don't pretend to know what they don't know and don't try to hide their intentions or tricks. They say we have this they mean it and if they say they don't have nukes for sure history has proved that to be the truth. They are like young sisters or brothers who look up to their brothers for all kinds of support and guidance. They are inexperienced and as such we try not to be strict with these only on that basis. We think they have a lot to learn just like how your young brother or sister would come and ask you questions. Our goal is to guide and protect these from the manipulating, cheating, trickery sisters or brothers who are greedy and want to grow at the expense of their brothers. We are for everyone, but I think with great powers a lot is expected of them too. We have seen a pattern incident after incident of trickery, abuse and no respect of the law. We have a bully or gang situation where the bully is using all kinds of weapons to rob the young brother demanding the younger not to make weapons but himself making weapons and pointing these at the young brother and demanding monies. The West in the last decade has jumped out of sanity and are acting like a bunch of mad wolves with nails in the brain with no one to pull them out or contain this madness.

xxvi. The West promised peace and prosperity everywhere for the past seventy- years but that has not materialized. Even the West now cannot afford to provide basic needs for their own populations recording high levels of poverty something not heard of in the developed world. So, we come in. There is a problem and doing nothing is not an option anymore. We are taking over the ship and changing direction for the betterment of everyone. Cooperate all humanity or you shall face our laws that close all loopholes which you have been manipulating for the past seventy years.

xxvii. Once again, we are neutral, but we seem to be strict with the West because the West is like an educated degreed person who has seen a lot and done a lot if this was our son we would advise and listen too. The developing world is like the daughter who had just finished A levels and about to start a university degree. These they need more guiding than say the elder degreed brother. So, if the elder makes a silly mistake you will be harsh with him or her because you would expect a lot from him or her as you view him or her as a role model to guide the younger daughter.

xxviii. It's not that we think the West is or not no, we know they are tricking and devious for self-gains and we know the reasons. The system has crashed and is obsolete so now they will never balance their budgets and will always have issues with debt, proper allocation, and global peace. We know why. They are wasting resources on obsolete functions that is why they are in this mess but don't worry we have the answers and the stamina to see our plans through but if you resist, it might cost you your lives as we shall not leave any law stone unturned until you have succumbed on your knees if not six feet under.

xxix. The New World is not for the short-sighted leaders who want a perfect eight in office. This is for leaders who want twenty-five global contingency plans and we are the only ones who can do so. Throughout the book, I will show you how the current institutions have taken the easy and cheap road. Make WMDs and kill as many if they are not part of us why should we care? Reversing everything and because of the huge aging base that depletes the government's finances then make these people age faster than normal and use digital agents and chips to kill them faster. The reason being that if we don't, we will have an older population with stagnating economies a receipt for disaster.

xxx.   I personally think we need to dissolve all these institutions and bring new ones that have time limits on any one issue. Say human rights or climate agendas which they can only do for say five years with their progress checked and based on merit can extend or be forced to apply for a different license say eliminating poverty. etc.

xxxi.   Countries like Syria must be forced to disarm maybe earlier as part of the global banning of weapons etc. and development packages offered to help with rebuilding with money raised from compensation claims, and the destruction caused by wars not prevented by the UN which they claim as their sole responsibility.

xxxii.   I am not against the UN I explained why I am strict with them. They are misleading the world and blocking any form of help. They are like impersonators a crime even now which carries severe punishments. They jeopardize the lives of women and children by pretending to stop the war carrying out investigations in which they claim nor to have found Weapons of Mass Destruction but then be unable to stop the war. What is the point then? We are putting new laws saying their presence is not for the good of the accused nations but to give a strategic hand to the invaders. What is the point of investigating even after not finding the weapons you still can't do anything? If you can't stop the war, then don't inspect and weaken others. Our new laws give the invaded or targeted nations a chance to self-preserve through a detailed analysis of the likely outcome and give them even grounds to arm themselves.

xxxiii. So why are we so strict when it comes to the killing of civilians mostly women and children?

xxxiv. The main justifications forwarded by all the governments breaking international laws are either national security or human rights abuses etc. or following certain treaties, etc. But to us, all these treaties are rendered void if they conflict with the peremptory norms of which the right to life and to self-preserve is the main one.

Section VIIIb

Peremptory Norms that can't be violated.

i. A treaty is null and void if it is in violation of a peremptory norm. These norms, unlike other principles of customary law, are recognized as permitting no violations and so cannot be altered through treaty obligations. These are limited to such universally accepted prohibitions as those against the aggressive use of force, genocide and other crimes against humanity, piracy, hostilities directed at the civilian population, genetic heritage discrimination, apartheid, slavery and torture,[15] meaning that no state can legally assume an obligation to commit or permit such acts."

Civilian Deaths.

ii. Any deaths of civilians are not permitted by law and there are no treaties or other laws that can override these. The first rule the right to life. Any breaking of these peremptory

51

norms which we have turned into direct laws will cause one to be labeled Hostis Humani Generis. An enemy of the people and as such can be attacked by the whole world. The idea is that such a violation can threaten human existence so that a person is punished by anyone.

Torture.

iii. This is the worst crime as it has slavery connotations as slaves were tortured to perform certain duties and favors e.g. sexual where they are degraded and humiliated first to be abused later. Torture threatens the fabric of international law as we stand firm against torture for any reason. There is no use of corrective behavior etc. as in dog training on humans. Such practices can only get one to be dragged to court.

iv. We must be very harsh on nations and leaders who think they can develop sophisticated drone-like devices for torturing people secretly. Express-command to put an end to this through our laws and courts as a deterrent. It is true here that evil can only breed evil both literally and figurative. Very harsh sentences might be a ground to deter and stop such an evil practice so that the world understands how bad it is. Sometimes the seriousness of the act can also point to the importance and serious nature of the initial crime. Some people can only understand that way they are born like that and change does not come easily. If it means the obliteration of the entire nation for the sack of global peace that can be an option. We are tired and fed up. Talking is cheap. The notion of action speaks louder than words applies well here. The international laws through the Jus Cogens; the peremptory laws declare that torture can bring global justice and punishment to your door and yet you carry on torturing people what does that tell everyone. I reiterate here that all the Jus Cogens laws invokes Article 1 that requires a global collective punishment. Express-command to put an end to this through our laws and courts as a deterrent. No other laws can override these and any actions that conflict with these laws makes that agreement or action void.

Piracy is the same as hacking in this case.

v. Express-command to put an end to this through our laws and courts as a deterrent.

vi. Some governments have invested $billions making chips to hack all its population at birth illegally. Implanting chips etc. reducing the quality and life span of its population as the metabolic processes are speeded up with the resulting aging of the population at a faster rate. Chipping and the use of remote-controlled radiation or electromagnetic frequencies can cause harmful effects to the body and therefore conflict with the first rule. The purpose of hacking is to change and cause modifications and at the end of death. Hackers are regarded as worst as pirates and as the slave traders before them and often regarded as Hostis Humani Generis as enemies of the people as they can destroy the gene pool and all humanity by playing God. Very strict punishment at the hands of the whole world. It applies here that an attack on one is an attack on the whole world and military action against such a country by all will and must be organized by Tomorrow's World Order as a deterrent and to set the record straight. We are tired of nations who think they are above the law. We shall swear by the assassin to do a great job. We don't want to take such roots, but some nations are begging to be annihilated. Change or we will change you apply here.

Slavery

vii. You will be shocked to find out that some nations are still doing slavery in the name of disguised protection, and the people threatened secretly through the use of chips and satellite technology to command and torture and reduce someone to slavery levels. The devices being used to give the people watermarks that are irremovable lowering the lifespan and quality of life as a population control mechanism a eugenic tool or a genocide stance if you ask me.

viii.   Laws to monitor activities of all satellites and checking and investigating slavery tendencies and any form of use of these to secretly enslave people. We are not suggesting using the satellite to put as surveillance but to check the satellite usage to uncover it is used to enslave and monitor people through GPS locality etc. Slavery can result in the annihilation of a nation and governments are urged to think again and trade carefully.

ix. Need for advanced ways of detecting hidden uses of the satellite. Implanting GPS can make one an enemy of the people and such practices have no justification whatsoever as they conflict with the right to life and to self-preservation as well.

Military action and international law.

x.   "The United Nations Charter requires a mandate from the United Nations Security Council for sovereign states to use force for the purpose of maintaining international security, but not for acting in self-defense or the protection of populations threatened by extermination at the hands of their own government. Since the UN Charter came into effect in 1945, military action in retaliation or reprisal to the act of another state has been prohibited; but a reprisal may be justified if its aim is to force the other states into compliance with its international obligations."

Section VIIIc

The E-Laws. The empathy laws.

i. Introduce new empathy laws. Take a new direction in law and start looking at the E-laws too; the empathy laws. These laws will help assess if the warmongers gave reasonable regard to the value of life of other people of different backgrounds. Usually, people would sympathize with people who have the same common ground as them

ii. It can be argued that those who cry for war at the expense of innocent women and children do so because they don't empathize with the victims in other words they give undue regards to the lives of 'remote' people but if one child dies in their country one they relate to they might end up killing the whole group of people who killed that child. This is human nature we are saying look both ways level the playing field.

iii. It's the fact that we are declaring that we are going to be all equal one day as such so we should assess if the leaders can give the same command if the to-be-victims were ones they empathize with.

iv. New laws to protect servicemen and women. It is now a law that military work shall be like any other profession where they expect to enjoy their pensions as well. Unnecessary military commands that put the lives of soldiers at risk will be illegal. Unlawful killing charges will be swiftly brought against leaders who negligently put the lives of people who took an oak to protect them. The idea here being that it's not just giving away their lives by taking an oath to die for leader and country but a hidden mutual belief that if I can die for you then you must be prepared to protect me as well and not throw me to be slaughtered by

55

insurgents or underestimated enemies.

v.   The burden is placed on leaders to do whatever in their power to avoid the loss of life. If a sniper can do the same job, then there is no need to get our best be slaughtered like dogs.

vi.   So, making an oath is as good as a bargaining stance for the leaders to do their best to safeguard the lives of these men and women. To add to this is sending people to war without proper gear or understanding of; local issues and the enemy-threat-level.

vii. Judgment in the-heat-of-the-moment can get you killed as a leader through the courts. Life for life applies in this case.

Section VIIId

To be the President or Prime Minister comes with greater responsibility and an oath is not a sacrifice but a direct command to do your best to save that life that offers to die for you.

i.   It is expected of any President or Prime Minister to command a method that avoids the deaths of these men and women.

ii.   To add to the above is the due care that is needed even after these men and women have left the military. It is a President's duty to make sure that they are safe and somehow provided for when military services have ended especially if wars have impacted them psychologically.

iii. Greatest crime to use devices originally meant to help them [In-built exercises devices etc. supposed that the soldier was a Royal Navy or Navy Seal and would spend 6 months in a submarine at sea, Surely some form of body aid would be needed for breathing and exercising as they are below sea and gravitation forces can cause health issues.]

iv. When the service is over these soldiers are mistaken for the retarded and all evil of society. Mind you these men took an oath not to reveal such secrets even to be labeled as such in the name of national security and protection of the President or Prime Minister or the dictator or Monarchy for that matter, but they did not agree for the same device to be used to damage them through hacking.

v. To be used to torture them or make them narcotic through continues shaking and rotating. These men and women end up in local neighborhoods where the local councils have no clue what means to take an oath to protect and honor. In military circles, your word is as strong as a bond yet the leaders to push political agendas to let local councils abuse these men of honor.

vi. Therefore, we shall put new tough laws against local institutions like the councils, hospitals, and police who take over or hack these men and women and to justify their jobs further abuse these people. These people gave their lives to this country and why let uneducated government instruments who are failures themselves abuse them. These people would fight even burgers to have a salary at the end of the month.

vii. So very tough laws to tackle evil local councils who are hacking all military men and women and use them as bait to attract more investments or justify housing issues. There must be trading places or sacking of these government instruments who are abusing our best boys and girls. Life imprisonment or even death.

viii. Hacking military men is a gross crime that conflicts with rights to life and quality of life. Hospitals and councils to be held to account and severe punishment.

Reduction of areas where issues are a problem as it only shows an unbalanced pyramid with more government personnel on top of few base people; drug users, homeless and muggers, etc. They end up using soldiers in return for food handouts and safe houses. Mind you these are the people who gave their lives to die for the leader and country and you let these people abuse them.

ix. The burden is on the President because the oath declared to protect him and the country after the service, he then has a burden to protect these men and women.

x. So, our laws will link these men directly to the President not necessarily the one who they made an oath to but any current or future President. This is one way to tackle this problem. If that means a special fund for the President or Prime Minister's office for such uses, then so be it. Instead of weapons and the military, these leaders have a burden of care of duty to these men and must allocate a certain percentage from the military budget to former soldiers and servicemen especially if the wars had an impact on them the more the funding should be.

xi. It is a President or Prime Minister's duty as well to raise money through donations for the servicemen who have left the war when still in office to this fund for ex-soldiers. Money is out there; people need to be reminded and be asked to donate.

xii. In the long run when all wars are a thing of the past the problem will subsidize.

xiii. The government must compensate these men and women in the case where there is a breach of contractual terms and where the information is withheld from them of what will happen to them as regarding this extra 'protection' especially when they end up being hacked by local hospitals and councils and used to drive local agendas. They were not told so when they enrolled and must be compensated, and the culprits brought to justice. There has been an abuse of power and trust. You should understand that in military circles a word or oath or contract is the greatest bond one can give and as such these men and women expect that bond to be respected and never be broken. If it's in local settings, it's a different matter how many times politicians have lied and retracted their comments. It's of little issue to them. To a soldier, this can be a thin line between life and death.

xiv. So, these people must understand and where the breach can be proved to be severely punished. This is a law that applies directly to the President's Office of Prime Minister's office because these men did not make an oath to protect abusive local councilors who don't even know what a war is. The oath was a bond between the soldiers etc. and the President that makes the issue one of the President's offices and should never be delegated to the local councils.

xv. Death penalty applies here it's a breach of trust that can result in the death of the soldier and as such the President or Prime Minister having a direct responsibility towards the welfare of these soldiers etc. must show that he or she does not allow abuse of the best men and women who not only gave their lives but are betrayed on his or her watch.

xvi. In countries where they are monarchies, soldiers are abused in the name of monarchies as they are tricked whatever is done to them is for the sake of the monarchy. These are lies as the monarchy encourage all citizens to report abuse even if they are not citizens. The monarchical rules or regulations advocate that everyone is equal be it a homeless soldier or not and should not be violated but to bring perpetrators to justice. Stiff punishment for those who would want to tarnish the monarch's name with lies pretending that they are torturing people to protect the monarchy.

xvii. Encouraging of all service personnel to log grievances through blockchain or other faster permanent ways that can save files permanently to be used. The reason being that most are abused being prescribed methods that damage their brain as therapy to forget the war-traumas but the therapy causing severe mental problems. Very strict sentences that include the death penalty as this breach the oath of enlistment.

Section VIIIe

Human rights violations.

i. We also have huge plans with human rights issues and how we can totally stop all the abuses that are going on right now. This is in part linkcd to the above issues. We want a world where there is peace, respect for human rights and the upholding of the rule of law. All our laws remove the triggers of abuse. Wars; - where leaders override rights to life and give orders to kill and then regret after office. We are and believe in pro-activeness and would not want unnecessarily killings or regrets, so we have banned wars and military interventions, etc.

Military Interventions.

ii. We have watched over the past decades and have concluded that military interventions only benefit the invaders who often benefit at the expense of innocent women and children and as such we have banned any military intervention for any reason whatsoever.

iii. Our challenge is for anyone to show us an intervention that did not result in the deaths of women and children? Mind you our laws put people first. We don't care if you provide the whole world with cheaper oil the questions did you get some innocent kids and women die so that you can provide that cheaper oil. There is a cost.

iv.   A human cost and the fact that you can't provide back the lives of these people make any gains useless because our laws will haunt you till death. Express-command to put an end to this through our laws and courts as a deterrent. We have devised a criterion to assess whether any military intervention is beneficial or not.

v.   Any intervention that results in the deaths of innocent women and children is illegal and can get the command issuer to be punished. Express-command to put an end to this through our laws and courts as a deterrent. The reason being that we might not be able to bring this leader to justice as we might see an invasion resulting in civilian deaths but nevertheless, we might send our best assassin. Through education, it will be easy because we will empower everyone to have a very high self-esteem that they will put themselves first and ban and close all loopholes taken advantage of that encourage bribery and make some people kill for money, etc.

vi.   We shall raise living standards and make one man stand for himself and only Tomorrow's World Order for everyone. Bodyguards and soldiers will not defend a rotten President or Prime Minister and might do us a favor and terminate that leader and use the right to a life of the innocent dead as the defense it does no matter that the dead are their enemies' kids and women. They are all protected by our laws which are global as we are a global leader not specific to any one country. So rotten evil leaders will be dragged to court.

vii. Our laws must be respected and above all life be given the importance they deserve. Express-command to put an end to this through our laws and courts as a deterrent.

viii. Everyone shall have the Responsibility to Protect the defenseless in the women and kids globally. It is irresponsible and arrogant to invade a country by claiming Responsibility to Protect those say chemically gassed and end up killing more women and kids. In most cases, the same countries that invade are the same countries for years that had brought the invaded country to its knees through sanctions that killed many women and children.

ix. To rely on humanitarian grounds will not suffice if you had weakened the people through sanctions. It's like the USA or UK fighting for sanctions against Syria and stopping any foreign aid that resulted in the deaths of women and children over the years then when the leader in self-defense gassed the insurgency with chemicals the USA or UK would then try to use humanitarian grounds or Responsibility to Protect the insurgency as excuses to invade. Such claims will only result in the USA or UK dragged to court for acts of aggression; for invading a sovereign country, undue regard to the lives of the women and children who died first through sanctions and secondly through the invasion with bombs spread everywhere, regardless.

x. Third charges of lack of empathy [E-laws] with the victims can be brought on top of that as one can prove that the sanctions and the invasions were imposed and carried out without due regard to the lives of the victims because the USA or UK lacked empathy towards the victims.

xi. In relation to the above, it can be argued that the USA or the UK has no right to intervene as their sole interest is personal for financial, strategic advantage or resources gains only in that everything they are doing is for personal interest other than the welfare of the Syria people.

xii.   They failed the litmus test regarding the welfare of the women and children whom they killed through sanctions over the years. Even if the sanctions were imposed by the UN all that is needed is to prove the fact that they created the UN and that the UN is funded by them through contributions and as such the UN is doing things on their behalf.

xiii.   They can never succeed on humanitarian grounds and Responsibility to act if at one point they advocated for sanctions that killed or even created hardships for women and children. It starts with these.

xiv.   It can never suffice to use humanitarian grounds to invade when you were harsh and lacked empathy towards women and children. How on earth would anyone believe you when you used sanctions to kill or affected the quality of life of these people how on earth can you sympathize with gassed rebels when you neglected women and children? Flawed is the word. Crocodile tears.

xv.   In such cases drag to court and use the E-laws to bring to justice for past sanctions imposed by these. Our laws make it easy to assess motives.

xvi.   You can't kill women and children and vow to defend a rebel?

Charges of looting indirectly or paving a way for multinationals to come in and take over after toppling of the leader result in misuse and looting that will disadvantage the local people and increase suffering and insurgents as disgruntling can be a problem. Charges of breaking the peace and interferences with a sovereign nation's affairs can be added on top of that. Recall in our world all nations are sovereign and nothing at all tampers with that. This is the critical point to us as all our methods depend on all nations being sovereign. Global emancipation of every nation on earth. On top of that impersonating and a false sense of security charges can be mounted onto that as well.

NEW LAWS II

Section IX

Oil drilling, fossil fuels, and alternative energy.

i.   Oil will never last forever even though it might be enough for our lifetime, but we must make sure that we lay the foundation and a way to come up with alternative energy sources by being proactive and not wait until it has run out.

ii.   If applicants meet our permit requirements, I think the drilling part is not an issue. Our laws in this area are to do with the side effects of drilling to the environment vis-à-vis the quality of life. Gas drilling can increase harmful gasses in the air and therefore laws must be in place to make sure that any drilling is safe and follows our laws and guidelines. Oil drilling and spillages can be detrimental to ocean life and wildlife and can destroy the ecosystem. Tough laws to deal with negligence, etc.

iii.   Drilling also means transportation by pipelines. We will need to check if the pipelines are away from densely populated areas and risks of exploding and fires are under control. Laws can deal with all these issues at local levels and national levels where they apply. Safety is the key here.

iv.   To reiterate our stance on fossil fuels is to ban these at a certain date in the future for use as the main source of fuel. Electricity will replace these even if we still have reserves. Vehicles, including cars powered by fossil fuels, will be a thing of the past.

v.   Honestly recent wars had oil as the trigger. Banning these fossils will mean a peaceful world. No pollution and very good quality of air. It will be illegal to use fossil fuels in buildings, vehicles, and machinery because the pollution will be way too much for the time in question. This will decrease the quality of life. Driving inside fossil powered cars will reduce quality of life, too breathing all that smoke and burned oil is no good. Life will be high, and a certain minimum standard must be met to rule out fuel fossils.

vi. Huge investments in alternative energies as a proactive measure and a better way of life. Renewable energies are cheaper and cleaner. All vehicles must have a renewable energy fuel source. All current cars that use fossils will be a thing of the past. Adoption of electric cars etc. or even better ones. Some materials will be banned from being used in vehicle manufacture, etc.

vii. Incentives search for alternative energies. Loans and capital made easily available provided by governments possibly through banks and these should be like depreciation that depletes in value with time to enable people to keep working on finding better alternatives.

NEW LAWS III

Section X

Globalization, Employment Creation and Job Opportunities.

i] It is a fundamental aspect of our printing money strategy that governments must go out of their way to make sure that they create and sustain new jobs and development otherwise hyperinflation will tear them down. Printing money without correspondent investment and development of industries and production can be disastrous. It is a law that the government creates and puts a framework that is easy for job creation and facilitates rather than stale development.

ii] The government of all global nations must remove complex bureaucracy and must ensure a simple process from company incorporation to operation to facilitate and promote huge production and development that is needed to avoid hyperinflation. This is a critical area and must be identified as such. Measures to provide state-of-the-art technology that is easy, fast, and transparent.

iii] Employment creation must be prioritized with every opportunity tried to increase jobs available and the actual taking of these and maintaining people into work by providing fast infrastructure and services like fast trains. It will be illegal to provide services like transport below a certain standard.

iv] It is our duty to make sure that we reduce global inequality associated with globalization. Our strategy of printing money will take living standards to a new level globally. We shall provide a framework and system to encourage networking and free movement of resources and labor, etc.

v] We shall devise a system that is comprehensive enough to stop and eliminate hyperinflation a problem with printing money. We have our own currency to beat that that is globally available, and we can give the nations affected by hyperinflation rights to use as they wish until they can use their local currency again.

NEW LAWS IV

Section XI

Section XIa

Sanctions.

i. Never to be heard of again. Banned. This is a cruel form, whether applied to individuals or nations. It's a cruel form of treatment that targets the innocent; women and children and kills these too. Individual's sanctions by state are banned and punishable under our laws. Sanctions are cruel and are used to make the targeted leaders, individuals and nations lose credibility and succumb weakening them as to get a favorable stance when bargaining. We stand against such barbaric, cruel, outdated ways of dealing with other human beings. We can bring new empathy charges to make sure that those who breach our laws will succumb to our laws. Trust me no one will ever get immunity when it comes to empathy. It's everyone's duty of care to every human being and imposing sanctions will conflict with the right to empathize with the innocent mostly women and children. We have laws punishable by death that emphatically prohibit reckless killings of women and children of any background. We will assess if you can do the same to those 'close to you' from the same background as you. If not, surely you will go down.

ii. I have argued throughout this book that the United Nations Security Council is the vehicle to implement the Colony Collapse Strategy. Since 1966;

iii. "The Security Council has established thirty sanctions regimes, in Southern Rhodesia, South Africa, the former Yugoslavia (2), Haiti, Iraq (2), Angola, Rwanda,

Sierra Leone, Somalia and Eritrea, Eritrea and Ethiopia, Liberia (3), DRC, Côte d'Ivoire, Sudan, Lebanon, DPRK, Iran, Libya (2), Guinea-Bissau, CAR, Yemen, South Sudan and Mali, as well as against ISIL (Daesh) and Al-Qaida and the Taliban."

iv.   [UNSEC].

v.   For the past fifty-three years, sanctions have been the choice strategy to induce discipline, and still, we still have the same issues since then. The poor developing countries are still powered if not worse. All sanctions have helped do is to kill the innocent and increase sectoral violence like in Iraq. The suffering of the people due to sanctions can be argued to be the trigger of the rise of terrorism in recent years. All that they are doing is provoke-to act the otherwise harmless nations causing all kinds of instability to justify future military action. The UNSEC through sanctions has been treating sovereign nations like school kids who deserve to be punished.

vi.   Our laws put emphasizes on state sovereignty and we argue that the UNSEC has no right to interfere with the actions of a sovereign nation. In our system, the UNSEC is under any sovereign nation in that the UNSEC was established by a few sovereign nations the big four whose goals and objectives they help to serve. The UNSEC has no peace in all its decisions and actions. For us as the global leader's international peace starts with sheer recognition that women and children must be respected and protected. Sanctions target these vulnerable people and use them as bargaining baits. Where is the need for global peace when you abuse the very vulnerable of any nation? We argue that this is a way of provoking the targeted nation to act in turn so that the UNSEC has jobs as now they would send peacekeepers, peace monitors, sanction valuators or implementors and above all inspectors who if the truth has to be said spies for the West Allis. This is a job creation strategy that lacks empathy towards the victims. But our E-laws to sink you down where you belong in the mud.

vii.   What is good if sanctions target deliveries with food and medicine for kids and women? What is good if sanctions block any aid and assistance towards a nation viewed as violating international laws? What is good when sanctions restrict financial, trade and commodities to a nation?

viii.   Sanctions, to be honest, are there to block any development. When a nation is about to lift itself out of poverty, they start talking about human rights in order to suppress that nation with sanctions. Sanctions block sources of finance, trade, commodities, etc. so that development is suppressed. A very hinge-pin theme of the Colony Collapse Strategy. It's a fact that sanctions are used against developing countries the very nations that need guidance and assistance.

ix.   We stand against such an outdated way of thinking. Our goals are to empower sovereign nations to be sovereign as the name means and help them move out of poverty. All these interventions etc. are stalling tactics so that they have jobs.

x.   The fact that sanctions kill innocent powerless people of any nation triggers Article 1. An attack of these weak powerless people for any reason let alone economic or political for that matter can alone call for collective punishment. We need to change the mindset and way of doing things. They talk about international peace as if they can do something about that. All they have done is give these women and children a false sense of security only to be killed on their watch. They initiate the attack through sanctions.

xi.   We are saying that sanctions are the first line of attack paving way and justifying whatever follows. Look what happened wherever initiated the attack through these sanctions. The sanctions killed the innocent and weakened the leaders as they are proved to be powerless that a foreign nation or body would deliberately kill their women and kids without them doing anything. A sign of weakness and see what follows.

xii.   They are then sent in to inspect but to spy and further weaken the local leaders. What follows this is an imminent attack killing even more people. This has been going on for the past 53 years. Today we say no never again. Our rules shift the focus from evil sanctions aimed to maintain the status quo in the name of peace. What peace? Whose peace? If you want peace, you do what we are doing. Ban wars. Make this a law. Ban weapons globally target those leaders as well who think are above the law. Express-command to put an end to this through our laws and courts as a deterrent.

xiii.   What gives them the right to kill other's families? If that does not work use empathy laws and drag them to court. If that does not work bring in the Colony Collapse Strategy argument. They are biased. Look at all their victims of these sanctions. The very nations who need guidance and help. Look they are sanctioning Iran on perceived nuclear proliferation, but the US has nukes, the UK has nukes, Germany, France, etc. and were these ever sanctioned for possession. What gives them the right to make and stock? Is this the main reason they are the ones destabilizing the globe through wars? Look at all the wars for the past 50 years. They are the ones at the forefront. We don't care for what reason. Has the US been sanctioned or punished for the Hiroshima bombs? So, based on this we think sanctions are a bullying tactic and as such these nations have rights under self-defense laws bearing in mind the threat they are facing in the US, UK, France and their backing power in NATO. It will be unwise for any of these nations not to think about getting enough power to counteract any attack. Under our laws, these nations are doing everything reasonable given the circumstances.

xiv. We believe and stand firm with the idea of the sovereignty of all nations and their right to self-preserve. The UN etc. have no sovereign powers and they can't stop any wars and talking about peace is an insult. A false sense of security as a deceiving tactic to block any help. Imagine if Russia or China wanted to help during the Iraq war. The presence of the UNSEC blocked any form of intervention to help. They might have assumed that this UNSEC was going to stop the war only to wake up hearing that women and kids were attacked in their homes. Where is justice? We are saying the UNSEC is the problem. Removing these and empower all these nations is the only way forward. Imagine years under sanctions and this means stalled development. These nations if the UNSEC is there will never become developed nations and will remain as developing. We don't want this. To stop this, we argued throughout the book that our laws will break even the mightiest nation or cult if we wanted.

xv.   Our goal is to get every nation to become very rich the only easy and cheap way. If we are to start printing money, we will not need any stalling tactic as we need full speed and firing on all cylinders to avoid hyperinflation. If we let a country be a target for sanctions that will mean the collapse of that economy. For printing to work, there must never be interference or too much government interference, let alone the UNSEC's. Above all, we will never tolerate the death even of one child or woman needlessly. It's best to drag these to court.

xvi.   Causing death by recklessness and lack of a duty of care.

xvii. Impersonating a body that can stop wars.

xviii. causing grievous bodily harm and unnecessary deaths due to sanctions.

Section XIb

Murder and manslaughter charges.

i.   They are targeting the weak and powerless and using these as bait and bargaining tools to weaken the leadership.

ii.   Colony Collapse Strategy as an act of genocide targeting a special ethnic group to wipe them as they see them as threats to their existence instead of peace.

iii.   Acts of aggression provoking a reaction to justify military action through sanctions. The idea here is that it is an evil way to anger someone by killing his women and children. These nations are forced to react as this is seen as a sign of weakness. It's the implied reaction we are concerned with here. This act of targeting someone's vulnerable and kill them at will.

iv. Enticing others to anger and war.

v. Inciting and triggering acts of terrorism. Under our laws, they can be punished for terrorist acts that happened to their people. We will extend punishment to include willful provocation in anticipation of such a response. In this case, we will treat them as themselves who have ordered the terrorist attacks and above all treat them as the ones who carried out the attack. Our basis here would be to assess the contributory factor here. If their acts trigger the terrorist act, we can treat them as the terrorist themselves in that the terrorist simply wore their shoes and did what they would have done anywhere so they are in the same position with the terrorist.

The E-laws.

The lack of empathy. Gone are the days when we turn a blind eye to acts that can be assessed under empathy. This is the only way to put an end to all this. I reiterate here that our laws see no differences even though we are different, but this difference is the reason why some things are happening the way they are. If we don't address these, then we will not solve the issues.

vi. Charges of stalling development and keeping the developing nations as poor as they are can be punished under our laws. We will use the quality of life argument. We are saying globally some standards if below a certain level will be categorized as criminally negligent and a lack of a duty of care on the part of the provider. So stalling development that affects quality of life can result in punishment as well.

vii.   Their inspecting acts can and must be viewed as weakening tactics exposing the leader and his people to the attacks of the West. Spying charges as they are no better than the U2 Spying Plane [U2 1960 Incident] Picture what happened during the Iraq saga. They weakened Saddam the moment he agreed on them to inspect. Their inspection which is spying meant that their findings were used to assess the strengths and opportunities for an attack.

viii.   Even not finding any WMDs they did not stop the invasion, so what was the point of the inspection. It can be argued that they should have done everything to stop the war. They did not even try to delay the invasion. Charges of unlawful killing in that they gave a false sense of security secondly they did not delay the invasion did not even rally support as such did not give the victims chances and time to escape worse because they entered Iraq and found no WMDs so people expected no invasion. But failed to stop the war. Now we are saying they meant deaths of these victims surely what was the point of inspecting unless it was a SWOT analysis?

ix.   Inciting the making of nuclear weapons or the need to possess some of the initiation of nuclear proliferation. Here we are saying that the sanctions created a 'need to act'. If it wasn't for the sanctions and hardship it brought, then there would not be a need for what follows. Our thinking here is that the targeted nation was not even thinking about say nuclear proliferation. But sanctions induced the need to do that on two bases.

x.   As a defensive mechanism. The targeted nation was

left with no option but to self-preserve, as it will be unwise of it not to start the proliferation as a self-defense mechanism or ii] as a deterrent even if they were not actually going to start the nuclear proliferation. The idea here is that the admitting of carrying out the proliferation is a way of keeping the threat at bay and away from the perimeter. It's like a scared person shouting that he has a weapon when he does not have any but to keep away danger from approaching. So, the nation is justified to do all this in order to protect its people. So, it is in no wrong, but the sanctions are. The triggers.

xi.   We are not saying sanctions don't work at all for the better, but we are saying the effects are more severe than the good they bring. Sanctions conflicts with all our laws. We don't and must not tolerate even the death of a single soul.

xii.   Show us sanctions that don't take any 21 grams and we will show you a way to use them.

xiii.   Sanctions make the UNSEC treat sovereign nations like kids who must be punished and told when to eat or sleep. This is a gross abuse and a lack of judgment and an act of aggression in that we consider this as slapping a lion in the face only to be attacked. That means you put yourself in danger and might treat you as suicidal or deranged of some sort. We can put charges of lack of judgment and self-harm. So, the UNSEC can be said to be putting itself in danger and if it wasn't of the presence of the 'other' in the West and NATO one of these nations might have done them harm. Again, we can say they are provoking others knowing that they have the backing of NATO, etc. Acts of aggression. Worse who on earth would deliberately impose something that kills the vulnerable unless it is to provoke or weaken?

xiv.   Another big issue is that of forced entry through the use of sanctions. Okay even though the leader invites them it is forced entry in that the leader does it on humanitarian grounds to save the lives of women and children dying. The time he invites them damage will have been done. His stance is a mitigation stance where he acts to reduce further deaths. It's not because he invited them willingly. He does that to save lives. So, the UNSEC forced their entry just like a burglar and I understand a burglar can be shot dead and the owner of the burgled house walk? Again, UNSEC's self-harm risk is evident. Lack of judgment to the risk involved. But because they are part of the gang the bully or cult, we can assume that it's an act of aggression inciting others to war. Acts of provocation.

xv.   Lastly but not list unprovoked gang attacks by the UNSEC who acts as the front line of the attacking gang going in to do a SWOT analysis checking the strength, weaknesses, opportunities, and threats. Collecting information and acting as spy planes before giving the go-ahead to proceed with the attack. Even if this was not their intention one can reasonably conclude that to be true. The thinking here is that UNSEC attacks the leader concerned through inspection weakening him even if they did not find the WMDs they will have left him for dead so that the others can attack him. They remove his defenses and highlight his weakness making sure that invasion is imminent.

xvi.   Zero casualty tolerance.

xvii. Too much power as a threat to peace. Belonging to a gang and the unbalanced threat in that all nations US, UK, France, etc. and NATO are ganging up on Syria, Iran or Iraq, etc. are like gangs that need to be broken down for the sake of peace. Their presence and membership to NATO is the main threat to peace and not the individual states they are going after.

xviii. I know most argued that collateral damage can be minimized and never avoided. NATO used this defense in the Kosovo war and justified their stance on killing only 400 something Sebs and 500 something Yugoslavs. Their stance is that a lot more would have died. We say enough is enough you spoil a gram of soul and we will spoil your gram too. If we are to go to war with sanctions surely now and day, we will. So, banned!

xix. I want you all to take this seriously and understand the origins of sanctions. Sanctions are based on an outdated banned military tactic that is meant to starve and kill anything that can help the enemies including women and children.

Scorched Earth Tactic

xx. A scorched-earth policy
' is a <u>military strategy</u> that aims to destroy anything that might be useful to the enemy when retreating from a position. Any assets that could be used by the enemy may be targeted. This usually includes obvious weapons, transport vehicles, communication sites, and industrial resources. However, anything useful to the advancing enemy can be targeted including food stores and agricultural areas, water sources, and even the local people themselves, although this has been

banned under the 1977 Geneva Conventions.'
[Wikipedia]

xxi.   Just like sanctions this scorched earth policy is meant to destroy food and water supplies with sanctions even medical supplies. This is prohibited by their own laws under the UN Geneva Convention. Article 54 of Protocol I of the 1977 Geneva Conventions. The relevant passage says:

xxii.   It is prohibited to attack, destroy, remove, or render useless objects indispensable to the survival of the civilian population, such as foodstuffs, agricultural areas for the production of foodstuffs, crops, livestock, drinking water installations and supplies, and irrigation works, for the specific purpose of denying them for their sustenance value to the civilian population or to the adverse party, whatever the motive, whether in order to starve out civilians, to cause them to move away, or for any other motive.[3]

[Wikipedia]

xxiii.   The idea is synonymous to the concentration camps where all resources are restricted or denied and women and children are left to die from hunger and disease as a military or political strategy to wipe-out or force the leaders to cooperate. Nevertheless, sanctions have the same aim as discussed above, to kill women and children to force those in power to surrender.

xxiv.   If a similar tactic was banned under their own laws why they still impose sanctions if they have the same effect?

xxv.   The idea of sanctions was used in relation to the scorched earth policy during the Boers wars even though the idea originated as far back as the Roman empire times. According to the historian and Labor Peer, Thomas Pakenham, Kitchener {created with invention of concentration camps,] initiated plans to:

xxvi.   flush out guerrillas in a series of systematic drives, organized like a sporting shoot, with success defined in a weekly 'bag' of killed, captured and wounded, and to sweep the country bare of everything that could give sustenance to the guerrillas, including women and children ... It was the clearance of civilians— uprooting a whole nation—that would come to dominate the last phase of the war.

         [Wikipedia]

xxvii.   You can see clearly that women and children under this scorched policy are meant to die through starvation to ' sweep the country bare that could give sustenance to the guerillas, including women and children....'. No doubt that the death of these is the main purpose of the sanctions.

xxviii. So, as such to apply the E-laws.

xxix.   Countries to be brought to justice under our E-laws for negligence and lack of empathy towards the victims. We must stop these leaders from inventing new tactics to still do the same practices that are banned.

NEW LAWS V.

Section XII

Section XIIa

Global Population.

i.   Our aims are to make people as healthy as possible. We stand firm against those who believe in the divine right or divine appointment that is they believe to have been chosen by God himself to act on his behalf. We are not against this just for the sake of it but only when the people involved start playing God. We believe God or the creator gave humans everything they need to search for solutions and find answers. We believe playing God in killing people to maintain the population to reasonable levels is plain wrong. It's the cheapest way to go about it.

ii.   Imagine God giving humanity all the brains so that he can kill? I always say you can close your eyes and easily kill someone, but you can't open them wide enough and create a human being. The easy things to do are always cheap and the wrong ones. They don't need anything. You can leave your brain at home and still do a great job. Surely this is not what God wanted assuming he is there. Imagine him creating you and everything only so that you easily kill? Does that make sense? Or he created you so that you become a God-like him too and create your own people who will work for you and make money for you or worship you just like we do. That is a challenge. It makes perfect sense. This is the idea behind artificial intelligence. Listen to the name; artificial intelligence. What does that sound like? If you are talking about this, then maybe I agree with the divine right of appointment. So, I agree God appointed some men to act just like him and one day find ways of creating their own people to work for them. Have you ever seen how some people spend their life worshiping a God they never saw? Don't you want someone who will trust you that much to dedicate all their life just for your sake? I think this is nearness to God. But I am not for 'trust' in that way. I think to some extent it comes down to slavery. I don't think God wants us to be his slaves. I think mankind has failed and just wants excuses. But I am not judging. So, our duty is not to kill.

iii.   We are against the government who make lethal bio-engineered, digital or cyber viruses to play God and wipeout people as during the bubonic plague, no.

iv.   We stand against governments making vaccines that will 'explode' say in twenty years killing 99% of the population for fears of population growth.

v.   We stand against governments chipping everyone illegally at birth as a medical record thing or for national security as a disguised plan to be able to kill at will, especially in the developed nations where most are old sucking all the resources without economic benefits.

vi.   We stand against governments making lethal mass murder weapons and testing these on others before granting them protection or donating or sending help.

vii.   We stand against governments provoking wars to get the soldiers killed to reduce the balance sheet bill and control the population.

viii.   We stand against governments False flagging in order to provoke wars or incite terrorist activities to justify wars in order to control the population. We are not against family planning and birth control if it's voluntary, but we believe also that the area is open to discussions as some nations can benefit from forced birth control methods if no one dies. Restricting pregnancy etc. can be subjective and open to debate.

ix. Our strategy is to match development to population growth. Instead of the easy way-out of killing, I think population growth should be a challenge. How can you provide for everyone without sacrificing quality? That's a challenge. Our goal as you know is to take living standards to never experienced levels before. Our five-year printing plan will help us achieve that. But to avoid problems with hyperinflation and stagnating development and unemployment etc. growth must be equal too. We must use new money to boost development. This can't be simply killing. We must create new ways of doing things and new services and infrastructure. We must grow and keep on growing to experience a huge shift from developing to developed or from developed to the very advanced. Growth should also be unseen before levels. We must find ways to expand and spend new money by providing new things. We must match population growth with corresponding service and infrastructure provision. This should consider quality too. So, we have endless opportunities that we are our only drawbacks. What level achievement we make depends solely on our inputted levels of thinking, dedication and manpower or technology.

x. The biggest problem is prioritizing here and knowing what is important or not. We can print $trillions but if we don't manage the money properly, we will still have problems and in the end, resort to easy and cheap ways of killing people. I think the fact that most are resorting to cheap killing ways is the fact that mankind has failed to think and priorities over the decades. Look now even with the huge population growth we are still spending huge budgets on military; okay this trick has worked in the past in that the weapons and military will eventually cause deaths of the people and reduce the population numbers through wars but now wars are a thing of the past. Look North Korea etc. are aiming for peace. We have banned wars and weapons, yet the military budget is high. Our argument is that we are wasting resources and mismanaging these. The only war that will result will be a nuclear war a big one as everyone, in the end, will see the need to kill each other as you might have grown to un-tolerated levels. But in this war, everyone might use nukes hoping to kill as many as can be as we will have gone maybe for centuries without global wars. This war will cause the end of humanity as everyone will throw everything in.

xi. So, if we make use of the critical needs first then the plan will work as we will stop wars. Weapons making and evolve the military in creating rather than destroying, etc. All other resources channeled to match population growth to resources and services, etc.

xii. Global population shifting can play a big role here too. We believe the problems with population are related to geographical areas as some areas are rarely populated while others are densely populated. If we provide opportunities everywhere people will be willing to relocate to these new areas. Globalization in terms of resources and people can play a pivotal role too.

Section XIIb

Encourage networking and cooperation to evenly disperse the population.

i.   Improve the quality of life, prolong life and reduce aging rates and punish governments deliberately aging their people to kill all early. Huge funds plowed into research and development to find cures, ways of stopping aging, prolonging life in youthful stages, etc.

ii.   Punish anything contrary.

        Nuclear Weapons.

iii.   Our stance is unmistakable we agree with current laws, but we think there is a lot of bias and deception on all parts. I think all countries must abide by international and our new laws banning nuclear weapons. I think all countries now admit to carrying out nuclear weapons as a bargaining tool to make deals to remove sanctions etc.

        All countries, especially the Middle East must take us seriously when it comes to nuclear weapons and stop any production or plans to do so. I know the current system isn't fair as we like it to be in that it encourages the use of nuclear as the situation is one-sided and imbalanced that one is left with no choice that it's better to die trying for them.

        This goes to all nations Iran, Syria, even the developed nations themselves. I think it is fair to leave a chapter to discuss this in more detail as this is such a sensitive issue often raised as a reason for opting for war and above all the developed nations own nuclear weapons but prohibits others from doing the same.

iv.   Nuclear weapons are weapons that cause massive destruction because the bombs release huge amounts of energy in exponential volumes that the bomb will cause extensive damage. A small bomb can destroy masses of the population with devastating effects lasting for years and as such are referred to as Weapons of Mass Destruction [WMDs].

v.   The law currently is selective with powerful countries allowed to make nuclear weapons and some countries banned to make these weapons. Some countries can have and test these weapons, and some are not. So, the current status of nuclear weapons depends on who is talking. Or put in other words, who is the boss.

vi.   All countries are banned to own, manufacture, test, produce, or process for the purpose of making weapons or for uses that might make it be used and used for weapons.

vii.   New laws to ban everyone under the sun be it the USA, the UK, North Korea, China, Iran, South Africa, Mexico, etc. I mean everyone is banned to deal with nuclear for the purposes of making weapons.

viii.   I will reiterate here that the time for ambiguity and selective advantage is over. Our stance on all weapons is to ban all and we stand firm about nuclear weapons. It is an offense to deal with nuclear weapons, regardless. There is no justification whatsoever in stockpiling these WMDs.

ix.   Total or absolute ban forever without any

reverting to nuclear weapons.

x.   No production of nuclear weapons and any WMDs.

xi.   No justification for making and using nuclear weapons or any WMDs.

xii.   No testing of nuclear weapons anywhere is permitted in oceans, land, air, etc.

xiii.   The nuclear weapons ban will be globally at a specific time.

xiv.   There is no country on earth that will make, use, keep, sell, produce, or test and be allowed to process uranium for the sake of making nuclear weapons this includes the USA, UK, France, Iran, Iraq, Syria, Israel, etc.

xv.   I think this is the priority of Tomorrow's World Order to make sure that the playing fields are leveled. We don't want the current situation where a few can be allowed through unfair laws not just to make but to go on and test these on humans. Something that must never happen in the New World. I emphasize that TWO will assess all past incidences and assess if the lives of women and children were killed due to undue care and what I can regard to as a lack of empathy if the same would happen in the country of the bomber and assess how they might react? I think it's fair that way. If they cry foul, then it's automatic that they are guilty. I think before going into more details I want to vehemently emphasis that we are in this situation because the current law depends on who is the boss who is talking, for someone or a country can break all current rules or override or replaces these rules with their own is a cause for concern.

xvi.   I think we must be responsible it's everyone's duty to make sure we all work together.

xvii.   There can never be a justification for using a nuclear arsenal for obvious reasons. Nuclear weapons are Weapons of Mass Destruction and they kill women and children. We have closed all loopholes that give leaders and those in power certain privileges and excuses say for using nuclear weapons to 'save going to war'. In the New World, this will never happen simply because it is killing women and children it doesn't matter if it is in another country of your enemies, for instance, etc. This is not a justification anymore and we will like I said to bring new laws that bring criminal cages to leaders and commanders who choose to kill say 200,000 women and children as to avoid a war. The deaths of these people will come and haunt not just you but your immediate family too for we have a life for life approach.

xviii.   To love your own is to respect others' as well. I think we have worked around all the international laws and closed loopholes people are taking to make nuclear weapons and use these to intimidate and frightened others to destabilize peace and security.

xix.   The crimes of aggression do not do justice enough here and we will go further and enforce other laws that ban acts that intimidate others leading them to want to make a nuclear weapon because the playing field is biased.

Section XIIc

Laws pertaining to weapons.

i.   Express-command to put an end to this through our laws and courts as a deterrent.

ii.   It is a criminal offense to make, authorize, give permission or command the manufacture and the use of any form of weaponry; missiles, bio-chemical, viral or even digital that threatens the rights to a life of others.

iii.   Any breach has an express given command to assassinate [orders of our courts]. Life for life or soul for soul and evil breed evil applies here. Such acts in the New World are acts that cannot be justified humanely and are believed to be a result of such genetic deformities and as such committing these acts can only result in one thing. Death by an assassin.

Iv.   Designing and patenting any weaponry is banned and prohibited whether you end up making the weapons or not. Thinking and encouraging the making of weapons if proved is a criminal offense.

v.   Every human being on earth should take care and responsibility to preserve and honor the right of life of his and others around him and such breach carries the death penalty. All current stockpiles will be handed to TWO who will dispose of them correctly and in accordance with law.

vi.   No arms dealing whatsoever. This also includes the manufacturing of vehicles or machines that can be easily used to pose a risk to life.

vii.   There shall never be rights to war and wars are a

thing of the past although the last world war (World War Three) can be facilitated by TWO to get rid of all stocks of weapons in case some countries refuse to cooperate. TWO shall and have made it illegal and a criminal offense to provoke others with the aim to incite a war. TWO is advocating for a networking and cooperation development stage and wars are a thing of the past. Express-command to put an end to this through our laws and courts as a deterrent. TWO shall enforce these laws through the use of assassins who will only target the leaders. People will understand that no matter what. The right to their life is priority number one. TWO shall encourage internal coups where the risk of death of our boys and girls is high.

viii. In such light, TWO will make it a criminal offense to encourage, threaten or engage in acts that create a situation that will result in a war.

ix. Such an act shall carry a death sentence expressly given. TWO shall give every nation on earth options and rights to raise grievances with one another and if after a certain time that can't be settled peacefully then an option of a 'Mother Of All Wars' is expressly given and that after that no one shall raise the need for a war and forever remain in peace.

x. TWO shall facilitate such wars with the aim to eliminate the world's weapons stockpiles before declaring wars as illegal forever. A two-year war period from 2020 to 2021 shall be given and in this period any disputes between countries will and shall be settled by war and after that, it will be a criminal offense to incite, urge or carrying out acts that will invoke or incite others to war. Simply because wars conflicts with everyone's right to life. Acts of sabotage or aggression that has a risk of endangering lives after 1 December 2021 shall be illegal and regarded as criminal acts.

xi. No country shall sabotage another or occupy another sovereign country for the need to incite a war. Any acts of sabotage to provoke others to war are criminal offenses and the leaders concerned shall be a target regardless of how powerful their country is.

xii. No one shall be above the New World laws. TWO shall force humanity to move away from defensive economies for the betterment of humanity. We are behind in the development process. The current crimes of aggression laws do little to put things right in place. First, it must be enforced by institutions created and run by countries that we are saying are breaching these laws and other international laws. These countries after taking what they want to blind the world then propose laws to pretend to safeguard others from further attacks. The institutions in place are like scout leaders with no powers at all apart from singing the Scout Motto. TWO is independent and unique with powers through our internationally sourced assassins to remove immunity from anyone and deliver instant justice. Anyone who believes in a New World Order that will take humanity to the next level of development is a TWO and shall be recognized as such and shall carry out tasks justly and as have requested.

Section XIId

We are justified under international laws to act on behalf of humanity.

i. Our laws are just and fair and for the sake of humanity as a whole and all commands to get rid of all violators and evil people who are against what is universally accepted are justified under international laws. This is within our rights as a global enforcer. We cannot be regarded as rebels. We are just introducing a better system that is for all humanity and we have a 'Responsibility to Act' and justified to intervene to save humanity from extinction potentially to be caused by the works of a few evil people. We can intervene on humanitarian grounds as well. The Jus Cogens norms gives us rights to call out for global justice where a certain people, country or cult breaches these rights automatically invoking international justice. Something we are now doing justified by international laws.

ii. Any missile or other weaponry testing is banned simply because it incites others to think about wars or to make illegal weapons in self-defense.

iii. No one shall be threatened, and it will be a criminal offense to threaten others (through missile testing, noises, sirens, etc.) hoping that they will buy your weapons or so-called protection for self-defense. These acts are not just criminal behavior but interfere with the right to peaceful life something I looked at above. It's not just a right to life but a right to a life free from interference, secret or direct threats, right to a life free from any unnecessary intimidation or psychological torture.

iv. Any institutions and people doing this are no better than muggers threatening with a weapon and therefore a criminal offense. Countries that act in such a way will cause uncertainty to the future of others and as such is a criminal offense. An intimidated and or threatened man or country can be a very dangerous man or country and causing such a state is a criminal offense punishable by death. These are dirty tricks to trick and corner others unjustly so that you have weapons to sell or a salary at the expense of others and rightfully a thing for the past. Cheap methods and shortcuts are and shall not be part of the New World. These people are greedy bastards trying to make a quick bark at the expense of others.

v. Banning of any use of any kind of weaponry to command others and get a response as a means of subduing others is illegal. Making and use of biochemical or digital weapons is illegal. There is no justification whatsoever simply because all these interfere with the right to life.

Laws to encourage networking and cooperation.

vi. Work together to ignore the physical boundaries between regions and countries. The whole globe should work together to encourage connecting the world digitally and physical through highly connected networks and much emphasis on the small passenger plane like forms of transport that travail in air easily from one country to another just as cars take people from the city to the other. Private planes' investment should be encouraged. Tele transporting is a possibility should be encouraged. People flying like birds from one place to another should be looked at. All the money saved from weapons manufacturers should and MUST be diverted into research and development. The globe; if not physically then virtually should be linked to encouraging networking. Borders and walls should be a thing for the past. Security and defense should be the last thing to come to people's minds.

Networking and cooperation should be the first. People should be able to leave their doors unlocked or share their houses with others for certain times when they are not home. The idea is to encourage traveling globally all the time with the need to just send a message stating the time and date you need to use their house or offices

Section XIIe

Prohibition of Intimidating and provoking fear as a law against bullies.

It is a crime to intimidate and unsettle others provoking fear leading to them thinking and acting on their fears to get involved in nuclear weapons and WMDs. I know current laws punish only those who end up thinking about nuclear weapons as a realistic form of defense. I want to point out that global peace can only come if we really solve the real problems. Our stance is straightforward banning all weapons and ban all countries from processing uranium or nuclear for weapons reasons be it the USA or Iran etc. I think the problem of today is that the Allies or developed countries of today are grouping to an enormous scale with almost all of them part of NATO leaving the small countries feeling vulnerable, marginalized and fearful for their lives as they can't match the other side's threat no matter what.

The lack of empathy connotations in the use of weapons in order to ban all weapons globally.

i.   It is our duty and right to level the playing fields and remove evil privileges that make developed countries kill without due regard to human life especially the lives of women and kids. This shall be a thing of the past.

Laws regarding the monetary system.

i.   I have argued throughout the book that the current system is now obsolete and must be replaced. I have proposed a new money system with our currency the Futuregoldcoin as the main global currency working side by side with local currency to boost economic growth while fighting hyperinflation. Read our Whitepaper in the appendix. We have a repetitive Five-Year Money Printing Cycle. The idea being that only new fresh money is the answer to all global issues we just need to tackle hyperinflation and all other issues regarding money. It's a win-win situation trust me on this.

NEW LAWS VI.

Section XIII

NGOs, Institutions and other bodies.

i.   New laws to control institutions and their operations. I have stressed throughout this book that most of today's institutions are there solely for job creation and to act as killing weapons or vehicles for such actions and without goals to solve real problems. The existence of the institutions depends on several suffering at the bottom. It's like a pyramid. If there is a large problem base, then it can support huge numbers at the top levels, but if the bottom has fewer numbers, then the top will collapse in. So, these institutions might be creating problems just to justify their presence.

ii.   So, as such, we have new laws dictating their operations. First for all to understand our stance and reasoning we emphasize again that impersonating a problem solver when you are not, is a crime as it gives people a false sense of security making them misjudge danger as they might trust in you think you have the stamina to stop say a war or prevent a genocide when you don't. These people if you were not there, they might have run and escape or look for help somewhere else.

iii.   To make things worse, their presence might prevent real helpers from acting, meaning their presence blocks potential helpers in that their presence gives them a false sense of resolve. They might assume e.g. in the Iraq war that the UNSEC was to stop the war after finding no evidence of WMDs. Maybe reason they did not intervene. But if UNSEC was not there they might have voiced a concern or delayed the war giving people time to escape.

iv.   We have institutions waiting for a huge salary at the end of the month and doing nothing but perpetuating the issues delaying so that they make a kill.

v. Some of these institutions, NGOs, etc. have been associated with political affiliations that they are now biased. They increase inequality etc. as they help only those with the same political ideologies as them, etc.

vi. Our proposals are to create a time limit for their operation in one area of concern. So, if an institution or body deals with weapons disarmament. They can only do this for five years and can only extend license based on merit of achievement. If they don't meet a certain level, they simply must give another body or institution a chance and they simply move onto the next problem say poverty or globalization. So, every five years their roles and focus will change until issues reduce. So continuous existence is linked and based on achievements and progress rather than by special privileges given by those who formed these institutions. This is the case with the UN that represents the US, UK, France, Germany, Italy, etc. the nations who form them and above all contribute heavily to them. The main reason we think they did not stop the war. Fighting your breadwinner, you can only end up going hungry.

vii. Separation of new institutions from cults like NATO, etc. and not linked directly to nations. Sources of funding should not be from the very people we are saying are needlessly killing women and children. Then you are not able to fight for the kids and children but will represent the views of the creators and funders.

viii. Stopping all impersonating activities as they can get the innocent killed clearly assesses the ability to carry out the nation's task or goal. A classic example is for the UN to claim to stop any wars and enforce these when they are like a church security guard when invaded will call upon

Jesus without doing nothing. You must understand that our value placed on life it does not matter whose life. What you can't create is holy and must be feared and respected. If you can't make life, then you can't kill life. If you can make life, then kill and create maybe we might understand but until then no killing. We are the voice of the voiceless and we shall punish killers of the innocent yet precious members of any society.

ix. Cruel provoking tactics of targeting women just like what terrorists do we make you be treated like terrorists and be punished harshly?

x. Most current institutions when they finally understand our laws and what will happen to them will voluntarily change or cease operation altogether. We have drawn a line, and it's not time to worship people who rack lives.

xi. If you say you are in the job of stirring development, then you must prove that and not do acts that conflict with your claims. A good example is when you use sanctions on everyone, yet you claim to fight for international peace. This is contradictory. This is what has been happening with the UNSEC. They provoke everyone and incite them to fight by killing their women and children and then talk about peace and removing threats to war when they are doing what they are saying to prevent. The minute they imposed sanctions is the minute they declare war on the sovereign nation they are dealing with. The very minute they breached international peace. To understand is one thing and to act justly is another thing.

xii. Future institutions must find ways of funding themselves. We don't want a situation where they don't stop the war as the UNSEC in dealing with Iraq then accepts a huge contribution from the US or UK. If you know the issue the UK owed the US World War II debt and if you look at the whole picture, it's like going to rob to pay debt and not stopping the war and then receive a big reward is itself a threat to peace. UNSEC can be dragged to court under our laws for conspiracy to rob, take by force through weapons, endangering the lives of the victims, and murder using trickery and undue regard to human life on top of that lacking empathy towards the victim giving them a false sense of security. Above that getting women and children killed for personal gains as the invaders are also their breadwinners. It will be unreasonable for them to stop their funder as payment will be withheld. So had no option and intention to stop a war on personal grounds. New laws new interpretation of the laws and bringing the culprits to justice. Change is imminent and inevitable. Are you ready to change and prepare to deal with our no-nonsense laws? We are not against anyone, but we must make you understand our thinking and the new approach to dealing with what we have called global evil and injustice. Be on the good side. Treat every kid and woman as if they were your own.

xiii. We don't know what situations where the West goes in and kill thousand women and kids first through sanctions and when Assad the Syrian leader attacks rebels then the West uses humanitarian grounds to invade and attack a sovereign nation. This is a thing of the past. We don't see the logic of killing the innocent and defend the otherwise crooks and muggers of any society. We don't treat rebels the same as civilians who are unarmed and powerless who have no one to defend them and most of all who have a huge heart full of faith and trust that they put their lives for you only for you to let them down and choose muggers over them. Be careful you don't want to be on the wrong side of our laws for we will eliminate you and all your bloodline. Respect the innocent and future people of any nation or face the consequences.

Regulating institutions and NGOs (continued)

xiv. New laws to control institutions and their operations. I have stressed throughout that most of today's institutions are there solely for job creation and to act as killing weapons or vehicles for such actions and without goals to solve real problems. The existence of the institutions depends on several suffering at the bottom. It's like a pyramid. If there is a large problem base, then it can support huge numbers at the top levels, but if the bottom has fewer numbers, then the top will collapse in. So, these institutions might be creating problems just to justify their presence.

xv. So, as such, we have new laws dictating their operations. First for all to understand our stance and reasoning we emphasize again that impersonating a problem-solver when you are not, is a crime as it gives people a false sense of security making them misjudge danger as they might trust in you think you have the stamina to stop say a war or prevent a genocide when you don't. These people if you were not there, they might have run and escape or look for help somewhere else.

xvi. To make things worse, their presence might prevent real helpers from acting, meaning their presence blocks potential helpers in that their presence gives them a false sense of resolve. They might assume e.g. in the Iraq war that the UNSEC was to stop the war after finding no evidence of WMDs. Maybe reason they did not intervene. But if UNSEC was not there they might have voiced a concern or delayed the war giving people time to escape.

xvii. We have institutions waiting for a huge salary at the end of the month and doing nothing but perpetuating the issues delaying so that they make a kill.

xviii. Some of these institutions, NGOs, etc. have been

associated with political affiliations that they are now biased. They increase inequality etc. as they help only those with the same political ideologies as them, etc.

xix. Five years of cycle for all institutions, charities, and NGOs.

xx. Our proposals are to create a time limit for their operation in one area of concern. So, if an institution or body deals with weapons disarmament. They can only do this for five years and can only extend license based on merit of achievement. If they don't meet a certain level, they simply must give another body or institution a chance and they simply move onto the next problem say poverty or globalization. So, every five years their roles and focus will change until issues reduce. So continuous existence is linked and based on achievements and progress rather than by special privileges given by those who formed these institutions. This is the case with the UN that represents the US, UK, France, Germany, Italy, etc. the nations who form them and above all contribute heavily to them. The main reason we think they did not stop the war. Fighting your breadwinner, you can only end up going hungry.

xxi. Separation of new institutions from cults like NATO, etc. and not linked directly to nations. Sources of funding should not be from the very people we are saying are needlessly killing women and children. Then you are not able to fight for the kids and children but will represent the views of the creators and funders.

xxii. Stopping all impersonating activities as they can get the innocent killed clearly assesses the ability to carry out the nation's task or goal. A classic example is for the UN to claim to stop any wars and enforce these when they are like a church security guard when invaded will call upon Jesus without doing nothing. You must understand that our value placed on life it does not matter whose life. What you can't create is holy and must be feared and respected. If you can't make life, then you can't kill life. If you can make life, then kill and create maybe we might understand but until then no killing. We are the voice of the voiceless and we shall punish killers of the innocent yet precious members of any society.

xxiii. Cruel provoking tactics of targeting women just like what terrorists do we make you be treated like terrorists and be punished harshly?

xxiv. Most current institutions when they finally understand our laws and what will happen to them will voluntarily change or cease operation altogether. We have drawn a line, and it's not time to worship people who rack lives.

xxv. If you say you are in the job of stirring development, then you must prove that and not do acts that conflict with your claims. A good example is when you use sanctions on everyone, yet you claim to fight for international peace. This is contradictory. This is what has been happening with the UNSEC. They provoke everyone and incite them to fight by killing their women and children and then talk about peace and removing threats to war when they are doing what they are saying to prevent. The minute they imposed sanctions is the minute they declare war on the sovereign nation they are dealing with. The very minute they breached international peace. To understand is one thing and to act justly is another thing.

xxvi. Future institutions must find ways of funding themselves. We don't want a situation where they don't stop the war as the UNSEC in dealing with Iraq then accepts a huge contribution from the US or UK. If you know the issue the UK owed the US World War II debt and if you look at the whole picture, it's like going to rob to pay debt and not stopping the war and then receive a big reward is itself a threat to peace. UNSEC can be dragged to court under our laws for conspiracy to rob, take by force through weapons, endangering the lives of the victims, and murder using trickery and undue regard to human life on top of that lacking empathy towards the victim giving them a false sense of security. Above that getting women and children killed for personal gains as the invaders are also their breadwinners. It will be unreasonable for them to stop their funder as payment will be withheld. So had no option and intention to stop a war on personal grounds. New laws new interpretation of the laws and bringing the culprits to justice. Change is imminent and inevitable. Are you ready to change and prepare to deal with our no-nonsense laws? We are not against anyone, but we must make you understand our thinking and the new approach to dealing with what we have called global evil and injustice. Be on the good side. Treat every kid and woman as if they were your own.

xxvii. We don't know what situations where the West goes in and kill thousand women and kids first through sanctions and when Assad the Syrian leader attacks rebels then the West uses humanitarian grounds to invade and attack a sovereign nation. This is a thing of the past. We don't see the logic of killing the innocent and defend the otherwise crooks and muggers of any society. We don't treat rebels the same as civilians who are unarmed and powerless who have no one to defend them and most of all who have a huge heart full of faith and trust that they put their lives for you only for you to let them down and choose muggers over them. Be careful you don't want to be on the wrong side of our laws for we will eliminate you and all your bloodline. Respect the innocent and future people of any nation or face the consequences.

xxviii. Surely you will never find loopholes to exploit because we have closed all. What you can do is dig yourself a hole in the ground and hide for our wrath will scorch the earth like angry fires and consume everything to dust. Be warned.

NEW LAWS VII.

Section XIV

War on Terror.

i.   Express-command to put an end to this through our laws and courts as a deterrent.

ii.   We are against all terrorists and are very harsh with these mainly because their tactics are barbaric and attack the very innocent people of any society. Terrorists are viewed and must be treated harshly as they threaten the fabric of our laws. Their acts of using women and children to push their agendas conflict with the right to life and self-defense. We are harsh with those who target those who can't defend themselves. Our first laws state that one has the right to self-defense. If you attack those who can't defend themselves, then you are the worst thing on earth, and we shall treat you as such. Here, the express command applies. I feel the same way with sanctions for the same reason because it's challenging us and what we stand for when you attack those; we are saying they can't defend themselves, yet our laws clearly state that they have the right to defend themselves. That shifts the burden of care and to acts onto us. To be the ones to defend them. So, we see this attack as a direct attack on us. An act of aggression to see how bad we can be. To us, terrorists and sanctions are the same as they use the innocent as bargaining aspects to be manipulated and abused. So, an attack on the innocent by terrorists will invoke Article 1 that says that an attack

iii.   But we believe some have genuine concerns as false flagging might have been used to provoke them but still killing women and children overshadows that we don't sympathize with them. Two wrongs don't make a right.

iv. Nevertheless, we shall provide a framework for addressing the real issues and misunderstanding of local needs, etc. This is one of the reasons why we stepped up. Some countries ' foreign policy has become a self-inflicting wound in that they have brought terror to themselves just for misunderstanding local needs and impersonating a global leader when you have your interest at heart. Probably the reason for the 9/11 attacks. I argued that a global leader must not be biased to avoid being regarded as an aggressor or an oppressor. This is true and we see the problems arising from this. You can't try to fulfill your own personal global policy and at the same time declare to have everyone needs at heart. It is just impossible hence the rise and worsening of the terrorist acts in the last decade. We must intervene and provide a framework for understanding, rebuilding, forgiving and simply cooperation. We always have the view and stance that global issues are too complicated to be easily solved by the current methods and institutions. We have come up with a different approach. That is assessing all sides. There is a problem, and that is a fact. To address the issues and act as the new global leaders is the only way forward. All impersonators are biased. They belong to cults like NATO with strict rules and articles that hinder pleasing everyone at the expense of the members see Article 8 of NATO. So, in that case, talking of global leadership is like slapping a lion in the face he will only attack you. A self-inflicted wound and putting yourself at risk and unable to judge scenarios collect therefore unfit to be the global leader and a peace monger for that matter.

v. Ban forms of protection in some countries confused or linked to terrorism in that this protect gives everyone express immunity no matter what the people can easily kill and are tortured as a way-out after being held for ransom and cornered to kill themselves and other. This is a medieval practice and we believe we should die with medieval times.

vi. Harsh punishment for government false flagging and outsourcing terror to pursue military goals laid out in long-term contingency plans. Use harsh punishment for leaders killing their people to justify wars this is not collateral damage but murder and if applicable a new form of genocides tendencies. Very harsh punishment.

vii. Our aims are to look at all angles and draw up comprehensive plans to deal with this so that we can start building again.

viii. Education in the form of affirmative information provision should be our goal. We are there to supply information and advice on the best courses of action to guide and lead as to avoid abuse and manipulation of these leaders after leaving office. Our laws will support and help people make sound judgments and prevent facing punishment in the future.

ix. It must be stated that some terrorist acts can trigger Article 1 that request collective punishment as attacks on the defenseless is an attack of all humanity.

NEW LAWS VIII.

Section XV

Research and development.

i. It is a law requirement that countries set aside a certain amount of their GDP as a percentage as funds towards research and development. Our aim and goal are to take humanity to another level never achieved before and only through research and development shall we be able to achieve that. This is one of the critical areas that need funds. We are going to ban a lot of things like reliance on fossil fuels and we shall need new alternative sources and only through research and development can we be able to do that.

ii. Doing nothing is a crime. Plans and evaluations of progress to be part of the system with monitoring and evaluation compulsory.

iii. Government to help provide a framework that makes everything smooth from obtaining patents and establishing companies, research, and development, etc. Laws that make the process simpler.

iv. Encouraging investment in this area through incentives, reduced taxes, and provision of state-of-the-art facilities, etc.

v. We shall provide a framework as a catalyst, a facilitator, a negotiator and implementer of things necessary to see this go smoothly.

vi. A global fund towards global research and development as well with a comprehensive plan that is linked to all levels. A global plan that recognizes national, regional plans, etc.

NEW LAWS IX.

Section XVI

Potential for World War III.

i.   Our concern is not just with the likelihood of a WWIII but with issues that this can be a nuclear weapons war were WMDs might be used from both sides to match the uneven threats with the West ever-growing in NATO and the Middle East resorting to nuclear for self-defense. That war can and might result in human extinction as the weaker outnumbered nations will have nothing to lose but to take as many as they can as they see their chances of self-defending themselves and their people reduced to nothing as NATO, the US, UK, France, Germany all group together to form a war conglomerate.

ii.   We shall aim to avoid any wars in the initial implementation of our laws, but we also acknowledge that some countries might want to throw in the towel after the last one for the road. In that case, we leave all doors open but for the sake of children and women will do everything in our power for peaceful endings. But the possibility of any resistance can lead to WWIII. But after that our laws will come into effect banning all global future wars and provocations or invasions.

iii.   If there is a WWIII our role is to make it as balanced as possible in case this initial one is unstoppable.

NEW LAWS X.

Section XVII

Section XVIIa

International laws.

i.   Effective dealings with;

ii.   Need for global peace.

iii.   Justice

iv.   Interest and finally

v.   trade.

vi.   Effective ways to deal with war crimes of past
        Disarmament enforcing our new laws

vii.   Banning of global wars

viii.   New laws to deal with terrorism and their financing

ix.   Dealing with crimes by state and corporates.

x.   New laws to deal with laws of the sea, etc.

Guns legalize or not.

xi.   This is a subjective topic with differing views on how
        best to approach this issue but nevertheless, I think it
        is clear and true also to say that legalizing guns go
        hand in hand with the democratic state and just
        society.

xii.   Countries, where guns are legalized like the US, are
        more democratic and advanced that issues like police
        harassment and brutality are minimum as compared
        to countries where guns are illegal to possess. I can say
        genetic heritage issues play a bigger part in countries
        where guns are illegal to possess. Police often take the
        laws of the country into their own hands and abuse in
        broad daylight and more often get away with what

would naturally be regarded as police harassment and brutality.

xiii.   A gun is a tool, a weapon, and a teacher in itself as well on how to behave. Imagine you are in a position of trust and you abuse someone unknowingly and a gun is pointed at you surely next time you will think twice of repeating the same mistake. It is a different situation also where there are no guns or other weapons, we find police abusing citizens something you would not see, say in the US where gun possession is legal.

xiv.   I say possessions of guns models the behavior of the society and more often removes situations of police harassment and brutality. I think societies that favor gun possessions are better on resource utilization as well.

xv.   Some poverty today is linked to time and money wasted on those in the authority where they ended up babysitting the whole population simply because they can when homelessness and poverty is an issue.

xvi.   In societies where gun possession is legalized these societies often are more productive as the special time and resources are not wasted on issues that can fall under harassment and brutality. Where guns are illegal often, the police have nothing to do that, they end up doing nanny's jobs instead of being put in the line of fire. When poverty is an issue no matter how rich the top leaders are or how much they feast on state banquets, the lowest man at the bottom detects the lines that must be followed. Countries or societies like these are regarded as unjust and undemocratic and more often corrupt.

xvii. The level of development of a society goes hand in hand with its views on gun possession. The less the restrictions the more advanced the society is. This is true. Look at countries like the US guns are everywhere and this sends a strong message as well as mess-about-abuse others and be taught a lesson. The law enforcers know this, and they will try to do what is best in the situation for everyone knowing that they can be killed at any time. The fear of death can also model not just the common man or woman but can command dedication and one's worthiness to the job. I am not saying that law enforcers don't get shot out of the blue, but I am saying that silly cases of harassment and brutality are scarce or non-existent.

xviii. It also produces better law enforcers in that they are vigilant as well and would not waste time on trivial things. Where there is nothing to do, we find law enforcers taking jobs like baby-sitting that would otherwise be done by social workers, etc. These law enforcers also end up using dirty tricks like torturing people secretly then taunt them knowing that less or nothing can be done to them. Surely that would be a different case if gun possession was legalized.

xix. So, I am saying that cases of torture are prevalent in countries with restricted gun laws like the UK than the US. Torture and restricted gun laws go hand in hand.

xx.   The more the chances of revenge attacks the better law enforcers become. The odds of fair play are leveled, and the situation is much fairer that in the end situations are addressed in a more democratic way than in situations where power is one-sided. Everyone needs to protect themselves.

xxi.   I have emphasized in this book that the first rule is the right to life and to defend yourself the rest follows from this. Self-defense is paramount and the gun laws show the status and advancement of the society. To achieve the level of development I am talking about requires freedom to protect oneself as well, and that includes freeing up gun laws so that each person has a right to defend himself or herself. I believe evil can only breed evil.

xxii.   They say guns don't kill people, but people kill people that is very true in that the level of advancement the people are in, the more the understanding and reactions they will have towards gun possession. In a democratic society, guns should and MUST be legalized. Whenever guns are outlawed such societies are often corrupt, undemocratic and very abusive that outlaws of guns help those in authority to create a hostile environment for everyone knowing that nothing can be done to them.

xxiii.   There is systematic abuse of human rights and torture is not just common but the norm. Torture is used to command and bully people in broad daylight simply because nothing can be done. If everyone had access to guns surely the picture would be very different. Countries that out-laws guns are undemocratic more often corrupt with only a few rich with the license to own one. Those in power are often corrupt and they damn know that if they were to legalize guns, surely it will be a matter of time before they are gunned down themselves.

xxiv. They are so bad they know legalizing guns will be like signing your own death certificate. So, I know you might be asking yourself; if gun laws can demonstrate how democratic a country is? The answer is that it's true. The more advanced the country the better the understanding that sometimes law enforcers are the greatest threat to self-preservation. Even in countries with strict

Death Penalty?

xxv. The death penalty can act as a hindrance to committing a crime. It acts as a deterrent to a crime. That being there is a deterrent to committing a crime punishable by death.

xxvi. It is being there that is a real educator that certain crimes can only result in death. The people make well-informed choices as they know everything. I am not saying that all the killings or crimes that will result in death can be logically explained but I am saying that the people committing these crimes are in a better position as they know this would result in death.

xxvii. In countries, without a death penalty, there are ill-informed moves that can happen simply because the person had no idea about the consequences. People might be tricked as well into slavery or committing a crime, etc. I found out that countries with express death penalties tend to be fair in their dealings with the whole issue than countries without a death penalty. I think there is justice to some extent because everything is transparent.

xxviii. Countries without the death penalty have a secret or hidden death penalty and as you will see later these countries end up tricking, manipulating, blackmailing and abusing the people. It's obvious every country has a death penalty the only difference being that some countries have it as part of the system and as a law whereas others tend to let you do them a favor to be spared or given some years. I think in these countries they have what I will call as protection here.

xxix. To explain the difference, I will explain the first and obvious death penalty practiced in countries like the US. If someone commits a crime punishable by death, he or she will go through the whole process of trial, etc. until he or she is given a death sentence after the trial and a date probably set. Then he or she will be on death row until the date has been confirmed when she or he will die. It's straight forward. I am not going to discuss whether this is fair or not here maybe later. The second situation is practiced in countries without an expressed death sentence but nevertheless has a 'death sentence'.

xxx. In countries like the UK if one commits a crime he or

she goes through the whole process until he is given a life custodial where he or she will spend the rest of life in prison. But there are other cases which I will refer to as protection. First, I will explain what is called initiation for you to understand this. Initiation is a practice of achieving a certain level in life and entering another level or joining a cult or established body with its own laws. To enter this cult or manhood the person must perform a ceremonial activity that shows he has moved to another level or achieved a certain level in life. Normally if joining a cult, the person is expected to perform a task that will show his or her commitment to the cult and as insurance, for example, he or she will do something that shows that he is wholly committed to the cause of the cult or group. More often whatever he is asked to do is often illegal in other words he has to surrender himself in exchange for membership of the cult. In normal circumstances, very few people would jeopardize their life forever for joining a cult, etc. It's just plain insane to lose your life forever for something that lasts a few days, weeks, years, etc. So, in most cases, people often refuse because logic always prevails. What often happens now is the fact that people are often tricked with the information withheld not being told every bit until later.

Section XVIIb

New Laws in relation to time limits.

i. No government or country shall abuse its own people by making viruses and loading their people as watermarks to protect important people or vulnerable people or in the name of eugenics, nor security nor population control. Making of any kind of watermarks-based viruses be it digital or cyber are illegal and continuing to do this when outlawed will result in the leaders being dragged to court.

ii. Express-command to put an end to this through our laws and courts as a deterrent. Viruses and watermarks reduce lifespan and the quality of life and treating people like cattle being stamped before a sale will never be tolerated.

iii. All kinds of protection are outlawed simply because they are prone to abuse and rely on a principle of scratch my back, I'll scratch yours something that can't be associated with any governments nor institutions, vulnerable people and people in a position of trust for that matter simply because most of the people involved are children and the vulnerable women. It is true to say that these governments deliberately starve their people reducing circulating income, making the benefit system very strict, deliberately so that people will 'scratch' their backs e.g.

iv. Children used to trap all untagged foreigners or used as prostitutes so as to trap the untagged so as to bring them in the 'system'. I remind you that the use of hunger or poverty is a form of torture as in the five techniques of torture and therefore an international crime.

v. This increases cases of child prostitutes as the children are used as bait putting innocent kids in danger if that means closing all these useless teaching hospitals and other government institutions so be it.

vi.   Very stiff punishments simply because these people are in a position of trust. Express-command to put an end to this through our laws and courts as a deterrent applies here.

Banning all time limits to bring a case to court especially where there is abuse by those in a position of trust or in power.

vii.   There shall never be time limits to take a case to the court that involves abuse by people in a position of trust like doctors, government institutions or teaching hospitals.

viii.   All cases can be brought to court at any given time by the victim or his or her representatives and it shall be free the institutions, governments, hospitals, etc. accused must pay for all court fees.

ix.   The current system encourages abuse after abuse by doctors and hospitals. To make things worse, the other government institutions then try to further abuse to silence the victim. The victim has no way of complaining. The hospitals won't look at the case after a certain time people even if you have compelling evidence.

x.   The High Court is very expensive mind you most of the victims have no source of income they are targeted with all governments making sure they only get amounts they set influencing managers, other income sources, etc. as all are illegally tagged.

xi.   The abuse by the doctors involves the implantation of GPS and devices they operate remotely. The first six months when the victim has a lifeline to take the hospital to court the institutions work very hard to make sure that the person will never save enough money to take them to the High Court. The High Court fees start at $600.

xii.   Commands are from the top and everyone will frame and do all the dirty tricks to make sure you can't bring a successful case to the court. The whole governments are corrupt, abusive and trickery. Tricking their people into modern-day slavery.

A hacker shall be treated as a pirate or slave trader.

xiii.   Governments hacking all their people are breaking the law. How on earth can a government load its people with radiation-emitting devices with GPS functions and operated remotely?

xiv.   Its genocide and can't be tolerated.

xv.   No governments shall be permitted to implant deliberately or indirectly secretly or otherwise for any reason. There shall never be any justification for such abuse.

xvi.   National security, dictatorship, eugenics, protection of the monarchy, immigration or other reasons must never override the right to life so these excuses will never exempt anyone from being punished for that. The teaching evil hospitals etc. a thing of the past as they are illegally operated because they are like assassins and drug lords taking everything in their own hands. How can those looking for organs also be responsible for the 'potential-donors' or own heroin fields to be prescribed to potential victims and above all be allowed to illegally implant torture medical devices? Speaking of grooming and cultivating for a benefit or profit. The so-called personal motive. Life must be respected.

Democracy.

xvii.   Global democracy by a certain date. I think the new laws and banning of wars and weapons together with evolving the military will solve most of the problems dealing with democracy. This must be globally developed or developing countries there are no excuses.

xviii.   All loopholes to be closed and violators to be punished with swift justice.

Decolonization by a certain date.

xix.   I think when the new laws take effect as self-esteem of everyone increases and people start realizing that there is more to life than worshipping others then and there will people reject any form of colonization. I think it will be irresponsible for former colonial powers to hang on to countries and land obtained by force during the colonial period.

xx.   New laws to make it illegal to keep land and countries obtained by force and unfairly. It's like stealing; to avoid any criminal proceedings former colonial powers will be given a time period, to return land deemed by all to have been taken unfairly or can sell it back at a fair price to recover some costs. Open to negotiations.

Use of secret slavery and viral be it digital or not to control the people.

xxi. A point related to the above point to see global · decolonization is the fact that some countries might want to cling to former colonies through secret slavery where people are forced indirectly to obey some acts against their will for fear of being further abused.

xxii. Very stiff punishment regarding anything to do with secret slavery

xxiii. or any unfair practices that have slavery or other forms of human degradation. There are no justifications whatsoever. I know in some countries they abuse people amounting to degrading treatment as part of initiation or protection.

xxiv. Be warned these rituals originated from a time when no one had human rights so listen to me and stop! It will cost you your life. Ask yourself when the rituals or protection of this nature first came into effect if more than a half a century ago stop automatically you are breaking the law. Change or we will change you.

xxv. Time and duration must be considered as well. A ritual that can be done a few times might be okay as the same ritual done over decades becomes gross abuse.

xxvi. So be careful to check time limits. Some acts leave permanent emotional and physical scars over a long period.

xxvii.

NEW LAWS XI.

Section XVIII

Section XVIIIa

Food and basic rights.

i.   You will be shocked that some governments even developed ones are using food and essentials like water as a weapon to control their population. Food is used as a tool to command people. We will fight for the provision of basic rights globally first.

ii.   Our strategy will make it illegal to override the first laws in favor of policies that make them starve their people. Above all, starving and intimidating your people is a form of torture and damn right torture is banned by international laws.

Climate.

iii.   I think most of our policies might be indirect but will have a huge impact on climate. Banning of weapons, wars, changing how the military work, banning of all fossil fuel consuming vehicles, machinery, and buildings, etc. will help tackle climate change.

iv.   Replacement of fossil fuels with cleaner ones, electricity solar, etc. Replacing all-metal vehicles with other ones made of recyclable material toughened fiber, etc. Research and development of better sources of energy. I think all these summits on climate change are a joke. You say zero-carbon reduction by 2020 and don't ban but increase fossil fuel consumption as oil-related vehicle production continues to increase etc. That's pathetic.

Useless institutions.

| v. | I think most of the institutions today are useless and are there only for cosmetics reasons i.e. to make the world look better and not actually be better and for other reasons which I will discuss at the end of the book. They are there to make it look like they are doing something, but the truth is that there are there just to create jobs compete with the world's poorest for resources. The world is in a state it is simply because you are there you bastard's competition with the poor. If you were not there, then we would not have all these problems. This is a troubling truth. |

| vi. | Most encourage poverty to justify their presence. We are going around this and ban some of these institutions. I think for most of these people who talk about human rights they don't even know what it means. There are so many human rights organizations in the world, and we have so many issues still problems, yet these institutions have been there for decades. |

| vii. | I will make new laws that evaluate the effectiveness of these institutions and close some that might be causing some problems we have. |

Increased risk posed by the presence of certain institutions.

| viii. | The reason why I am against useless institutions is the fact that they put lives at risk. People when they see the number of institutions and organizations that claim to offer help, they can get the belief that there is help there when most are |

just paper pushers with no ways of helping at all. I think most are for 'cosmetics purposes' only put there by the very people we are saying are breaking our laws and other international laws to keep people quiet.

A job creation strategy at the expense of innocent victims.

ix.   I argued above that it is a common strategy of some developed countries to create lucrative jobs at the expense of the poor. It can be argued that developed countries, for example, might create a problem through say invading a country and planting landmines so to render the land useless. After some time when the landmines have done some real damage through deaths and maiming then the land is devalued. Once that happens, they then send their multi-national companies or other branches like the Red Cross to remove the landmines at exorbitant prices thereby creating jobs and lucrative markets landmines can be removed at 1000 times the cost of planting.

x.   I will reiterate here that laws to assess for a lack of empathy aggravated decisions will be done and if it can be proven that the decisions if maliciously given without due regard to life. Our aim is to be fair and to deal with evil according to law.

The E-Laws: Lack of empathy connotations in all cases.

xi.   It will be a law that crimes that are considered as cruel are to be assessed if they can be said to have lacked the empathy element. I think this is a great step towards equality, reconciliation and rebuilding the world. This will act as a deterrent to future crimes and will make people think again before committing crimes. Again, if a person is breathing by any means through a machine or not has to be held accountable for any crimes committed since the day that person was born.

The age to be tried for crimes.

xii.   I think I personally learned this the hard way. Imagine a kid making a silly mistake that ended up costing his life at 17 years old. I think this is a debated subject, but it might be wise to increase the age of responsibility. Open for debate.

Global Health.

xiii.   A very sensitive area but one that we have sure plans. Our current system has gone bonkers. It's humanity's inferiority to do what is going on globally with the health sector. I personally think it's time we take a turn for good.

xiv.   The current system is against all our laws and not only conflicts with our first rule but contradicts our laws so we can't work with this obsolete system. Full stop. There is no negotiation at all. Crash the whole thing to the ground with immediate effect and replace most. The current people if not lazy then they are very complacent and if I have my way drag all to court. How on earth can you recreate the worst time in mankind's history? How on earth can an institution trusted with the health of everyone be making and using viruses be it biological, digital or cyber ones just to create jobs by recreating the worst epidemics and the war conditions to justify existence?

xv.   I mentioned above that the current health system globally is obsolete and must be replaced with immediate effect. The health system was created during the war or soon after and as such they try to recreate those conditions so that they are viable and justifies the huge budgets. Can someone tell me that life expectancy and the health of global nations are the same as seventy years ago? Not the same obvious so would you not expect the health sector to change? I know this for a fact that the health sector especially the hospitals have diversified taking other roles which were currently not for them.

xvi.   The hospitals in other countries now compete with killing agencies like the CIA. In some countries have become the vehicles of the death penalty themselves caring out the executions taking things into their own hands.

xvii.   The sad side is that these hospitals or the health sector target fathers who they regard as weak who they 'assassinate' as most are illegally chipped at birth and they can't complain because all court lifelines had expired by the time they discover that they have a needle electrode up their ass by then it will be too late already marked for death at birth. Why one might ask? So that these institutions look after the orphans through teaching hospitals who run day by day robbing banks to reward orphans who obey and listen but punish those who refuse. That brings me to the use of torture.

They practice torture.

xviii.   You will be shocked to know that our public health competes with gangsters for heroin customers and they even have their own heroin fields. To make things worse, they implant chips that are remotely operated to all children at birth which they later remotely operate torturing the orphans as behavioral change therapy. Just imagine how bad it can be if no one knows and believes that these kids are being chipped at birth and imagine the kind of torture when no one can prove that they are chipped? Do you also know that the same hospitals prescribe heroin?

xix. I am 100 percent against everything our public health system stands for. They are going for short cuts kill rather than create.

They are involved in child grooming.

xx. The orphans of dead fathers are looked after by the hospitals who take over as guardians providing for the orphans teaching them to bet on say horse racing where they have the control as horses can be chipped to control energy levels. In return, they link through the chips to potential buyers' or people who might take them as wives, or they might end up as prostitutes being tortured and told to go and meet someone the hospitals might want to get tagged. So, in fact, it's the hospitals that are training prostitutes to use as bait. We know agencies like the CIA used the same techniques to get to some people including politicians, etc. If they refuse these kids are tortured until they are taking their heroin as a prescription. In the end, they are disposed of to keep the whole issue a secret.

The public health sectors have become the worst hackers.

You will be shocked that the hospitals use James Bond gadgets to spy on everyone globally. To make things worse, they breach trademarks or patents rights by stealing the person's designs and falsely claim to be behind that person's success but what they are doing is using a video or screen sender linked to a chip implanted at birth to spy on everyone and then follow those who might be working on something. What they do is use the screen sender to monitor whatever you do, what you watch or who you call on your phone. Behind your back then stab you in the back blocking your meetings or clients until you accept that they are helping and in this case, they damage something on your body, eye or make you age faster as a mark that you belong to their 'cult' or whatever.

Gross breach of human rights. A hacker is as bad as a slave trader Hostis Humani Generis and as such an enemy of what we stand for.

xxi.   Hacking and implanting chips at birth etc. all is against what we stand for. There are no justifications whatsoever simply because all these gadgets, chips, etc. are operated remotely and have GPS functions that mean they use radiation and other dangerous waves. All this is against the first rule and all reduce quality of life amounting to gross abuse. Imagine someone in a position of trust with a joystick in the hand stimulating the genitals of your wife or child for that matter? Gross abuse.

xxii.   Express-command to put an end to this through our laws and courts as a deterrent is appropriate here because it's either kill or be killed in the end because the goal of a hacker is to change, modify, damage and in the end cause malfunction of an otherwise healthy system or body. Against the first rule; the right to life. How can you have a life when it's in someone's hands and in most cases someone who despises you? Express-command to put an end to this through our laws and courts as a deterrent. Track and trace; new roles of our military or organizations like NATO as an 'evolving task'.

xxiii. 6. Our public health is involved in eugenic thinking. Okay, I am not against the development of perfect genes but if you are the ones causing the bad ones in the first place, then it becomes a different issue. The chips implanted to all people in developed countries can be remotely operated and be augmented by further needle electrodes or diodes to stimulate nerves in electromagnetic stimulation and tampering to or obstruct many bodily functions like egg production.

xxiv. They are deliberately causing genetic defects to create more jobs and justify chipping kids at birth but remember the chicken or egg scenario here. What came first? Is it the egg or the chicken? If they can influence egg production and if it takes say for argument's sake four days naturally and if they make your body produce an egg in two days are there chances that the egg might not be ready or deformed or lack something that if fertilized might lead to disability? Take me seriously here. What makes then expects to look at the number of disabilities especially the obvious ethnic population that is obviously chipped at birth as population control in certain countries? I know there are arguments that people like Asians they marry their cousins so say if people with the same genes if they met, they might have a baby thereby increasing the chances of genetic defects. Okay, but could it be the fact that the chipping on population control could be the main problem here. Over history, people married a close relative from the Roman empire why we didn't have so high cases of disabilities than recently. Not documented? Not good enough reason. Something is going on. Is this another chicken and egg thing?

xxv. I think we need new laws around this. We need a clear and transparent system where everyone illegally chipped at birth must be told and give consent and chose to be clean of all chips. There must be investments in the technology that overcomes these issues. There must be machines everywhere that can check if people have been violated by being chipped without consent and are used as bait or abused or their systems tampered with.

xxvi. Very stiff penalties resulting in death simply because radiation is no friend to humans. It's irresponsible for the governments concerned and the leaders if they can't justify these acts must be dragged to court. Express-command to put an end to this through our laws and courts as a deterrent. They are no better than a mass murderer, a person who commits genocide, etc.

xxvii. Laws to ban such practices unless if the person is advised of the risks and agrees. This is no different from slavery and as far as I know, slavery was abolished many years ago. In most cases, this is for population control where the government chooses who to kill and choose when they die.

This is true in countries without the death penalty that everyone is put on 'death row' on birth by being secretly chipped and that chip is used to control the life of that person and how he or she will die. Simply because people now live longer, and the government knows the population is old and will do real damage to the balance sheet.

xxviii. Stiff laws to outlaw and ban such practices even criminals do not deserve to be treated this way because you have committed a crime equivalent to murder the day you chipped that kid or person. It will be possible to bring charges against these doctors on self-defense ground in worst-case scenarios, but everything must be through the courts. You can justify this on grounds that they are trying to kill you attempted murder from the day they implanted that chip.

xxix. It will be a law to kill in self-defense if the person has done an act that violated the first rule; the right to life and to self-preserve so a person can defend himself or herself. Remember this is because that the chips are planted to act as killing weapons through the use of radiation emitted secretly by these chips. So, the doctors are murderers as well who must face the law too.

xxx. More serious issues regarding the making of digital, cyber or biological weapons for the hospitals to remain viable. You must go to your doctors for digital weapons that might be used on you to drive attendances? To create and use these weapons as they lower quality of life in the long run.

xxxi. Ban all companies making this kind of stuff. Close all universities' departments involved in producing all these stuffs. Express-command to put an end to this through our laws and courts as a deterrent. Drag to court all leaders approving such practices simply because the acts conflict with the first rule they are like murderers.

xxxii. Involvement in terrorist acts. The command givers and drivers behind this using siren to direct just like a film director. Listen to sirens they coincide with critical points of attacks etc. can't be a coincident. I discussed this in earlier and later chapters.

xxxiii. Yes, you will be shocked that through what the hospitals call protection they are recruiting and training all terrorists we know today from 9/11 hijackers, etc. all chipped with gadgets that are controlled by only people in a position of trust. Yes, the chipping is used to torture pulling eye iris causing great pain and stressing life until the person finds a way-out through revenge. The targets have themselves been put through a grieving stage or tricked into committing a crime then blackmailed to revenge by killing innocent people. Again, care to be taken here ask yourself what came first the chicken or egg because they might argue that they chipped the person because they suspected him or her as a terrorist but maybe they made him or her a terrorist. It's hard to believe that a person who is chipped like most of the 9/11 attackers can escape the radar of those who have access to these chips. Do you know the teaching hospitals train people to be prepared for say terrorist attacks and what are the chances that on 9/11 we had a group of firefighters rehearsing when the 9/11 attacks occurred to check the firefighters who filmed the first plane hitting the Tower? Check also in UK the 7/7 attacks happened when a group of people were rehearsing as well see the film Loose Change for details.

xxxiv. I think the whole system has tarnished once was a respected profession to the lowest of lows. These people are supposed to be trustworthy and honest. Imagine them hacking your items and pretend to be clever and teach you how to run a business when their profession is about wiping the elder's buttocks. It's pathetic. It's bad judgment they are not qualified as managers to run a business. If you want business ideas, you don't go to teaching hospitals but to managers, universities, etc. Most of the problems we have today are a direct result of this abuse of trust and power. They are not afraid simply because literally, they have a joystick in their hands to control everyone remotely like operating a drone. Imagine the bad aspects of technology? But we shall put new laws and swear by the assassin that he or she will do a great job to clean this mess.

xxxv. Huge investment in the technology with the military who are used to kill now forced to look for answers as well. Tracking and tracing all kinds of shenanigans.

xxxvi. Cyber-attacks by the hospitals as they have access to billions of medical records through these chips. A new threat and a risk to humanity a cyber nuclear electromagnetic attack or bomb can be used to wipe-out everyone with a chip that is all people born after a certain time having their devices switched off some even blinded as the chips can hide the iris in the eye-socket preventing vision. A cyber electromagnetic bomb or attack is a new global challenge. What is happening with humanity is that when we win over certain threats like biological bacteria and viruses, then these people create digital versions taking us back to the beginning? Now we have the same threats but different versions. We start all over again, wasting time and resources when we should be looking for other things to enhance human life.

xxxvii. Very stiff punishment to these people who would create deadly threats to mankind. To hell with them. Stop funding anyone developing digital threats or other new forms harmful to humans. Open your eyes and see that we are going in circles. In truth, we are still in the medieval period when the black death was killing people only that we have substituted the real pathogens with digital ones, and we are trying to recreate those scenes, so our public health has something to shout about. That's not just evil but makes these people Hostis Humani Generis people fit to be attacked by all nations without any mercy.

Hostis Humani Generis.

xxxviii. Tomorrow's World Order will have express authority to finger a country to be ganged-up-on by the whole world if they pose a real threat to everyone's future.

xxxix. I will have the power after investigating any nation to get it attacked without need to bring the matter to the court simply because a person or country that practices evil at such levels will have people in the courts as well to manipulate and stall progress buying time may be to destroy the whole humanity. We can't take chances we just need to convince other nations that this is happening and if a certain number concurred, then there is no need to consult that country but to act swiftly. Look what happened to Hitler. No one decided to take him to court because people were afraid that he might kill more before he is stopped and as such, we will do the same. Some chips like I said can threaten the survival of all humanity. Some countries chip everyone in the name of protection to safeguard their way of life. But say in case of an electromagnetic bomb that explodes all chips we might have total wipe-out and human extinction and as such, I think if it can't be proved otherwise, I think that can automatically make a country or their leaders qualify to be Hostis Humani Generis.

xl. Such acts of chipping everyone can result in human extinction who knows what technology brings tomorrow and the fact that this is done secretly raises grave concerns. Here it's not just laws that need to be enforced I think that can justify isolation of that country on the grounds that it poses a threat to all mankind and as such, all its people who are chipped might be prevented going abroad until investigations prove that these chips are not harmful to others. As the chips can be cyber electromagnetic bombs. A point in relation to the above is the fact that such chips are used as weapons to mobilize anyone who might come near them. This is true as the chips are used to trigger a defensive mechanism that immobilizes others by blinding them as the chips can be used to pull the iris of the eye and hide it in the eye-socket rendering others prone to attacks putting life in danger and as such can be said to conflict with the first rule. Think of a car immobilizer that instantly stops the car. Okay if for safety reasons this can render say an attacker immobilized as he or she is blinded by the chip but what if the chips are used to rob people or trap the whole world all getting blinded so that you are forced to sign your life away in exchange of your sight? If you refuse, then you are killed or forced into slavery or prostitution or to become even a terrorist? Who knows the real intention?

Section XVIIIb

Equality.

I have no doubts that once the laws are into effect, we won't have problems with equality. We are working very hard to change current laws that make it easy to break some issues that matter to us. The wars, military, and weapons were a major issue conflicting with all other issues we have today, but all these are gone or will be banned so I think once everyone's self-esteem has reached higher levels, we will automatically treat others, respectively. I think it's a fair statement that the abused are the people who abuse too. The idea of ball-rolling applies here. They are abused so that they abuse others. Those shown love at earlier ages are more likely to show others love and respect. This goes beyond just talking about equality we must look at this issue in broader terms. Addressing other areas as well but I am not worried about this. It's something that comes naturally once we have achieved and solved other issues. We will see.

International law and justice.

i. I think our laws represent international law and we will work very hard to make sure there is justice in this world. We are not creating laws that people don't know about or never heard about. We looked at the common problems and then assessed why we have these problems. We also checked if we have international laws that support these issues. The truth is all our laws are there in international law, but we are rearranging and prioritizing certain principles, making things that are believed to be the norms now; right to life and self-preservation as priority laws and paramount ones that must be observed first and never overridden. Currently, there are other laws that can easily override these laws and people easily find justifications and get away with that. So, what we have done is to remove these other laws or areas that give people in power reasons to override these laws; the major one is the military, wars and security reasons. We have protected all future and current leaders from persecution when their term in office has ended by removing the need to commit crimes in the name of self-defense. When your term in office has expired, you won't need to be blackmailed by these teaching hospitals into signing your life away or the life of a close relative no. You can enjoy being a great leader and be remembered as such.

Migration.

ii.   Our aim is to create one globe with no walls or boundaries where there is one dominant currency that works side by side with a country's own currency to boost wealth and growth to encourage free movement. I think the differences would be the amount of the fee's countries would like to charge for entry as we would like to make sure that there is some country autonomy left. The only restrictions might be due to the fees payable as we would like to encourage competition as well. I think this is another area open to discussions as it might be good if decided by each country if they know this is the networking and connection era enough of building walls.

Peace and security.

iii.   Banning weapons globally and wars are great strides towards achieving global peace. I think it is highly correct that we have been talking about global peace for decades and yet we achieved none. So, as Tomorrow's World Order we have come up with laws that will be observed globally to change the way we do business.

iv.   I think the whole world must evolve and everyone must do what they have never done before because change is coming, we will ban all useless activities and monitor these institutions and recommend other areas that need looking at. It's not a dictatorship but as I have argued we must use all resources wisely and work at optimal capacity. Read this together with 'Useless Institutions' in later chapters.

Population.

v.   I think this is an interesting topic because it raises a lot of questions and this makes Tomorrow's World Order differ from all current institutions like the government and its hospitals and the killing squad and even the New World Order.

Laws relating to the Middle East.

Political and religious instability.

vi.   The Middle East and the Persian Gulf are the worst culprits in this regard. Unnecessary killings and fighting of different sectors for religious grounds etc. must stop. We understand the fighting goes back to the AD era and to be honest we think education and change of beliefs and attitudes and self-empowerment will play a crucial role than just laws. There is a need also to look deeper into the root causes. Unsettling issues remain that make the whole thing a hard task nevertheless we are for global peace and that is what we are going to achieve. I think understanding and coming together to work together and compromise some aspects for the sake of peace will be pivotal. The fact that they rely on books written centuries ago in the Quran and bible etc. is a challenge to be viewed and solved with great caution. I understand one of the issues is regarding prophecy.

Prophecy.

vii.   I understand whatever is written must be fulfilled if it hasn't been. That creates a problem. Whatever decisions you can make today have little bearing as at the end of the day prophecies will play a bigger role. I understand they follow two sets of leaders one for the

Shia and the other's Sunnis, etc. That could be the root of the rift and an everlasting one in that they have to fulfill the prophecies of these leaders who predicted that these two sets of people will fight each other for a thousand years before only one of them is chosen at the end of the day. So, in that case, sometimes the people fight and refuse to compromise as to fulfill these prophecies.

viii. I also understand that whatever is in the books must come true, so they do what was written centuries ago even if it is not irrelevant now? Could this explain why wars and sectoral violence is never-ending? Now you can understand why I explained our stance as to religion the main reasons why I used the bible and Quran to explain world issues as well.

ix. I think religion is a sensitive issue that needs understanding from all perspectives to find common ground for peace's sake. Nevertheless, that is not a justification for wars and as such our laws apply globally and we may be very strict with nations from these regions. We don't discourage religion but if that is the reason for wars then we need to change people's perceptions and understandings.

x. I argued that the heavenly life in the bible and Quran is a state we must achieve here on earth one day. People need to believe that too and work towards achieving that. What I like about our laws they are universal.

xi. There is no one who doesn't want peace and the best life has to offer. I think you need to compromise and lose some beliefs and gain some too. If Allah and God are for peace, they would not want to see sectoral violence. We have all we need and shall sacrifice other aspects like investing in wars and weapons, etc. This money shall be used to uplift the lives of everyone.

xii. Some living standards and services shall be declared

below standard and institutions, governments, organizations, etc. providing these be held to account and be forced to provide better ones.

xiii. Once education [not academic] but spiritual and psychological has been delivered, we expect people to change and have high self-esteem to believe that life is worth it and no one shall be a suicide bomber, etc.

xiv. Need to provide here on earth everything people they wish to get in heaven. Beautiful wives, virgins, loads of wealth and simply peace of mind. There was in the past so much violence with bombs going on non-stop. This is a criminal offense as it impacts heavily on quality of life. First, encourage development. Military money to be used for the betterment of humanity. Life must come first. No foreign nations to manipulate oil resources at the expense of the locals.

Better living standards and the elimination of poverty, etc.

xv. Religious leaders to play crucial roles in educating people spiritually to give everyone hope. Stiff penalties for stirrers of violence to destabilize these countries.

xvi. We have banned arms, so no arms deal, etc. a first step to keeping and maintaining peace.

xvii. Development programs aimed to alleviate poverty and increase literacy skills and above all provision of best infrastructure. Dubai led the way instead of using oil revenue on weapons they should improve the quality of life of their people.

xviii. The West has been a very bad role model and if these changes in the future the developing countries can learn one thing or two from them. The idea here is to facilitate global networking and cooperation. Education in warfare tactics and general life should be taught as most fall in the West's psychological traps of trusting people who have been evil to them as far as they can remember.

xix. If they can kill women and children through sanctions, then they are no good to you. The Persian Gulf leaders [PGL] must understand the West. If they use force and group together into cults, then they are no good to you as well. You can tell the PGL will not even defend their own people.

xx. These leaders must face our laws. Apart from being the victims of barbaric abuse, they do nothing for their people. If a businessman can defend what is rightfully his by owning a gun license, why let others invade and rob you killing your women and children too. I personally think the equal and opposite force is lacking and if left like this will only result in human extinction. If you can't change then better group. An Asian equivalent of NATO is welcome even though we will be banning wars and weapons they can evolve. They can lead to finding a better alternative to fuels, even better, they can invest in cyber and digital defense, etc. There are so many areas to get involved in.

xxi. We can ban all wars and weapons but still, it does not mean the end of the military. My main idea is that these people are success-driven and determine to find what they set to do. We need them but not killing people but being the leaders if you like development. We can use their technology for human development.

xxii. Fighter Jets can become for private use. All the advanced gear and gadgets can be used for human development, so the military is still viable, but they must evolve and whatever they do being for the benefit of humanity. What is even better is the increased salaries? Why channel money to huge weapons etc. when you are out of pocket. We change people's perceptions. More money for you. Meaning incentivizing people and ask them to create solutions and lead the way. It will work. I have faith in them.

Responsibility to Protect their people.

xxiii. They have a greater responsibility towards their people, yet they just go by the floor and get millions of innocent women and children killed needlessly. We shall also drag them to court for impersonating a true regime that will protect their people. It's not just a matter of sitting and waiting to be the next in the line.

xxiv. They don't even challenge illegal invasions or call others for help. We have others who can help those who have a Responsibility to Protect their people if the invasion is for personal gains.

xxv. We believe they are neglecting their duties to their own people. To protect them at any cost and defend them. The fact that they do nothing puts everyone at risk. We are against recolonization and we will use our powers to avoid some governments enslave the world again. So, there is help all they need to do is ask. We are saying we can bring the same charges as we do to the invaders. They have given their inhabitants a false sense of security. They might hope they would trade oil for support and help, etc.

xxvi. Our laws give everyone the right to defend themselves and their people and resources through force as well if invaded.

xxvii. Foreign invasion is banned by all laws and there is no justification whatsoever without consequences.

xxviii. Lack of the duty of care to the women and children where they did nothing to prevent deaths of women and children when sanctioned instead just seated and waited until sanctions had killed many. Education is vital in military strategies. The West is a formidable force to be reckoned with simply because they have grouped into a cult in NATO. Why not do the same for the sake of your people?

xxix. Value your life and start thinking as if you are on earth to stay forever. Change the mindset that kills people's hopes and giving them fear and hard life that they wish they killed some to go to a place where there is peace. Self-defense is your right. Especially considered what you are up against.

xxx. It is a reasonable excuse to arm yourselves and group as well with real nuclear weapons. The world is unfair anyway. If the USA can use some nukes on Japan and get away with it, why can't you use some to defend yourselves in the worst-case scenario? [NB we are going to ban use of all anyway WMDs, anyway. Just an eye-opener.] It's illegal to use WMDs.

xxxi. It is irresponsible for a government to let others kill their own children and women without international calls for help. Iran should and must not be another Iraq. We don't stand for anyone but for all hence one man for himself TWO for us all. The fact that the aftermaths of wars are worse than before invasions make us take a different stance. We have realized that affordability is the root cause and our method will change global politics as we know this today.

xxxii. We shall lobby globe-response to armed robbery and unfair killings of women and children. No women and children shall die at our watch and without severe consequences. Our laws will clarify international laws and remove any ambiguity or loopholes being exploited e.g. humanitarian grounds. These will never stand with our laws especially if the invaders have a shabby past and have no empathy for women and children of different backgrounds.

xxxiii. We believe an attack of innocent women and children is an attack of all mankind that triggers Article 1.

Section XVIIIc

Terrorism.

i.   Very strict with these. Tough sentences as well. The main reasons are that they kill innocent women and children as well. They use these as bargaining bags as well. That makes us not even have sympathy with them. All these people are protected by our laws and an act on civilians is an attack on all humanity and can lead to global collective punishment.

ii.   Death penalties as well for anyone who kills women and children. I don't care for what reason. They might have been wrong okay, but two wrongs don't make a right in that way we must treat these as enemies of the people too.

iii.   Ban all terrorist activities there is no justification whatever. Be strict with governments that support or incite others to terrorism. This means banning acts of provocation where the innocent are killed or oil looted so that they revenge the attack. In such situations, if the other side can prove that you deliberately provoked them to use terrorist acts to revenge then you are like someone running and attacking a lion and getting mauled you can't blame anyone but yourselves.

iv.   These would be treated as self-inflicting wounds. All the other party needs to prove is the fact that there is a cause-and-effect relationship. The initial act is the main trigger for the terrorist act.

v.   Had they not killed or looted in the first place none of this would have happened? My main base for this stance is in line with the psychological games of the West. Mind games to deliberately create situations that justify military action. It's like killing with a missile the innocent women and children say in Afghanistan and when the Jihad retaliates and carries out terrorist activities, then you are to be blamed.

vi. Even though they are dragged to court and using our laws to punish them you too are dragged to court for self-inflicting wounds. For aggressive acts that put the lives of your own people at risk.

vii. More charges of endangering the lives of your own people and putting them at risk will be leveled against you. We will further go on and claim undue regard to life for personal gains. You are in the same position as the people who attack themselves just to make excuses to attack others.

viii. To us you are a threat to global peace and as such must be severely punished and labeled unfit to rule and run any country. No other national security laws can override these laws and we will have banned all other justifications for not putting the lives of everyone including your enemies first.

ix. Severe punishment for leaders doing this attacking oneself is not just a disease but gross evil that can threaten human existence in that these people have no fear and one day might use nuclear weapons that will kill even their own people for personal or selfish gains.

x. The greater the risks of using nukes and WMDs as they are not afraid to sacrifice their own too. Death penalties apply here. Evil with evil applies here as evil can only breed evil. Severe punishment for false flagging. This is a common practice to get others attacked on false accounts. It's not just evil but irresponsible too and puts innocent lives at risk. Dirty tricks can cost lives.

xi. Tough laws outlawing any direct or implied false

flagging as to unfairly attack normally powerless people in order to rob or impose inhuman degrading treatment or revert to colonial times. This applies globally, not just to the West we have Persian Gulf countries doing the same.

xii. Clearly, state our laws and provide these through advanced ways e.g. blockchain system that is fast, or a centralized version that can easily be used for everyone to read and acknowledged the knowledge of the laws.

xiii. There will never be an ignorance plea as an excuse after the laws are published. It is everyone's responsibility to make sure they are familiar with these laws and have read and understood them.

We do our best to link everyone globally and provide a platform for interaction, cooperation, and negotiations.

Global peace is our must and everyone's responsibility and a breach of law to incite others or cause instability very strict punishment to deter. Laws to ban situations where some dodgy leaders would try to sacrifice their soldiers to reduce the military salary bill or sending troops in war zones without proper gear from that specific zone. Slaughtering charges can be brought against such leaders. Every family of soldiers who died this way to receive compensation with a need to prove that.

xiv. Burden is on the government and the President or Prime Minister to ensure the welfare of the soldiers. The duty of care or Responsibility to Protect is derived from the oath which is a request to do the same as they offer to die protecting these leaders and country. The leaders and country, in turn, must reciprocate and swear to do anything in their powers to show gratitude toward these men and women. In this case, compensation would not be enough.

xv. To discourage taking advantage of the situation first; use them for political propaganda or to drive local budget campaigns by local councils and then compensate them after abusing them very strict laws that include the death penalty. These soldiers were prepared to die for the leader and the country who ever abuse them must be willing to die for them and the country. Like for like to apply here. These men as we saw fit shall be the responsibility of the President's Office and not some local councils who don't know what the military stands for.

xvi. A word and promise in army circles are every soldier's assets something to put your life on and breaking or betraying this trust carries severe punishment. Local authorities to be trained to understand this as the only way to a solution. Providing housing and food handouts is not the answer probably a third type error. Solving the problem but with the wrong solution as good as not solved.

Section XVIIId

Laws relating to African Leaders.

Africans Leaders.

i. The same issues apply globally but Africa has its own continental problems and I will look at it here. African leaders as low-level threats concerned about self-governance rather than international inclines. African leaders and other countries are regarded as low-level threats with little or no potential for global military attacks as what the Middle East rich in oil is perceived as. As such the UN's judiciary system in the ICC is left to eliminate these low-level threats in the Colony Collapse Strategy, which I advanced at the beginning. Most countries in Africa are poor by global standards with most are regarded as developing nations.

ii. No wonder their problems are specific to Africa with dictatorship, corruption, genocide tendencies, tribalism, poverty, and instability the main issues.

iii. These nations need foreign assistance to topple the dictator and this gift is the same to be used to topple them and get them dragged to courts by the ICC on weapons charges or use of force or genocide and war crimes after being given weapons by the West.

iv. All our laws will apply globally without cherry-picking.

Banning of wars and weapons purchasing here applies.

New laws to deal with dictatorship and the need to solve the real issues. New ways of recording and safekeeping of war crimes. Use of the blockchain as well where necessary to collect and process or keep evidence to be retrieved later.

v. Our laws to life and self-preservation applies here too with stiff punishment for breaches, etc. Finding ways to tackle corruption, poverty, illiteracy, etc. Encourage development packages and aid to boost progress and networking. Money saved on military and weapons to be used for research and development poor industrialization of farming whatever improves life and later education to be used to boost self-esteem etc.

vi. Religion and other political and tribalism are major causes of wars and we have ways to deal with these. As basic needs are met, the less people tend to fight. Most of the fighting is for basic needs when others are spending huge sums on weaponry, etc. They say a hungry man is an angry man, and this applies here.

Strict laws on genocide and its prevention. With stiff punishment for culprits, etc.

vii. Empowerment of governments against the West who might choose to test their man-made viruses on them in exchange for food handouts or weapons. Poverty can influence the decisions to take and the national policy too. Development packages would be beneficial. All sanctions to be banned and never to be used for any reason. Countries that offer conditions that mimic sanctions will face international laws and any unfair practices with colonial connotations or slavery to be dealt with swiftly.

We don't like to witness situations mimicking say slavery or colonialism no.

viii. Military training in warfare tactics can be beneficial although the locals are used to destroy their own leaders through food bargains etc. with some people in Africa will go to lengths for handouts selling their own people for advantageous situations and benefits, etc.

ix. Crimes of humanity and aggression the two main trappers of most African leaders committing these through fighting to remove the dictator and themselves be taken to courts etc. Very strict laws to prohibit the acceptance of any military favors in terms of weapons etc. mainly from the West as these will be used to trap them and get them killed.

Human rights.

x. Nevertheless, just like any other country human rights abuses are prevalent with leaders forced to opt for other issues overriding the rights to life, etc. Another major issue is the lack of democratic situations that allow people to freely choose their own political inclination.

xi. Laws to encourage freedom and rights to choose freely, etc.

xii. Lack of the rule of law

xiii. No upholding of the rule of law and the need for new laws and support toward achieving that with extra funding for the provision of basic needs. More accountability to be demanded and laws put in place to deter this. Training can benefit some while some are unredeemable.

Tribalism.

xiv. This is specific to Africa with violence and unfair civil wars resulting in the deaths of women and children. Our rules apply here too and reckless and undue regard to innocent lives can get the leaders to be dragged to court.

xv. Aim to eliminate factors causing all these tribal conflicts. If education both academic and tradition might be beneficial and encourage everyone to some form of compromise and sacrifice for the betterment of others. Any causes of divisions to be addressed and a lasting solution is found to stop this fighting.

Torture.

xvi. Torture is a problem in Africa with the good part

being that the methods of torture are still primitive that leaves marks etc. and can be easily proved unlike in developed countries where it is hard if not impossible to show evil hacking as the source of all issues. With the right technology that is still a possibility. So, African torture cases are easily collected and for such reasons, people have easily seen scars that can be used to push for justice.

xvii. But this presence of evidence in form of scars has made African leaders refrain from torture because they might be taken to the court that has meant high genocide rates where people are killed with bodies hidden away from the view of people. We have advocated that even though the African leaders are still corrupt and favor dictatorship, we think the ICC is not-fit for purpose due to the bias and targeting of African's and since 1945 bring only African's to trial and letting others get away with murder.

xviii. So, ICC is biased and represents the views and goals of the West who created and funds it. Whatever they do so is in the interest of their investors the West and the very people we are saying that they are breaking international laws by targeting ethnic and carrying out ethnic cleansing of killing potential threats who might one-day group and form wars.

xix. Drag the ICC to court for ethnic cleansing and being biased with aims to eliminate future leaders to reduce the likelihood of wars.

xx. Charge them with bias and targeting attacks against the Africans and putting lives at risk as they drag them to court to be further abused. Reluctance and powerless of these institutions to solve global issues compounded with lack of a military wing all acts against them.

xxi.   Look at the source of weapons in most cases they are a gift from the West and bring charges to the country involved for supplying weapons that are used to kill women and children and therefore the source as such apportion blame.

xxii.   Add the E-laws as well to prove that they lacked empathy even though they knew that weapons were to be used on women and children. They must have anticipated or foreseen this coming therefore aware but acted negligently and lacked empathy towards the victims.

xxiii.   If personal gains through sales of guns if not given as gifts, then advance on E-laws that they preferred profits over the lives of these people simply because they are remote to them. You would not sell or give guns to someone who might use them on your own women and kids, would you?

xxiv.   Our laws will punish everyone involved and especially the real culprits the weapons supplier. If there were no guns easily available women and children might not have died in such numbers.

xxv.   Change all laws relating to this. Add a lack of empathy with the victims by the West who offload weapons cheaply or unjustly knowing that they will be used to kill these. An accessory to murder.

Section XVIIIe

Laws related to Global empowerment and emancipation.

i.   Our policies, regulations, and laws are there to make every country here on earth take the bull by its horns and be responsible for their own growth. All nations on earth have this ability and can grow all that they need if education and balls to do it despite all fears and discouragement. This is the reason why most countries have their own currency apart from the Euro nations and that can explain the stagnating growth and the recent recessions and all the problems with the Euro something I will look at below. Our aim is to educate and empower all nations.

ii. Our goal is to increase living standards and draw a line at which no one shall fall below in terms of the standards provided. It's all in your hands and don't look to anyone else and don't be tricked by handouts and don't be oppressed by sanctions as we have banned all these dirty tricks to keep a few controlling everyone.

iii. Sanctions are banned globally, and people should not be oppressed by a few countries. We stand against all this.

Drastic change of government attitudes and fiscal policies globally.

iv. Our approach is to change and emancipate and encourage a new way of thinking even if our methods are not perfect in the short run at least we know what they have been preaching for the past seventy years and that that does not work.

Printing and printing and more printing as the only way out of poverty and not debt.

v. The saying that forever indebted to you applies here very well. The idea of a government is for it to be indebted to its people. There are there to serve and increase the value of the people. Printing money rounds after rounds injecting the money into the economy to boost all kinds of development.

vi. Printing will only increase development and growth. It is a fact that the only growth just like in a human body is through huge food intakes. If you want to grow, you don't limit food intake. You keep growing and taking nothing out and keep eating common sense. All today's policies by the IMF etc. are only to keep the poor poorer.

vii. Every nation on earth has the potential and ability to become a developed country or to grow even further simply by printing more money or eating more food.

Section XVIIIf

Never Fear Debt.

i.   Debt should be part and parcel and your major attribute if it's internal debt one you can manage. We are against any form of external debt in that it has a high chance of sovereign risk. Borrowing abroad will only put you at risk of being attacked if you default and that conflicts with our first rules; the right to life and to self -preserve. The idea behind this is that countries or nations that are prepared to lend to anyone have more power and are a threat to you. This is the reason why they lend to you in the first place. Mind you externally very few laws relate to international debt. If it is to lend nationally, then take the person to court if he defaults. If it is a foreign nation that borrowers and defaults, then you have no courts to deal with that. What can the lender do? Very few courts to deal with these issues. Countries that lend like the USA and the UK only borrow because they can use military force on those who they are lending to in case they refuse to payback. They are more a threat with nukes which they use to guarantee the return of the loans. The US is the largest lender use this notion to its advantage and can easily lend knowing that any default they can sanction or attack the defaulter.

ii. We are against such practice because this gives the US the right to make nukes and use these nukes to guarantee the return of the loans. Hell no. We are talking about potential human extinction and using nukes to force countries to pay back loans is not just irresponsible but a threat to humanity, global peace, and justice.

Our policy and aims.

iii. We are going to ban all international borrowing. Why borrow and pay heavy interests and unfavorable conditions when you have a God-given right simply to print and at the same time boost the value of your people. Every time you borrow globally you are lowering the value of your people and making them owe you instead of you owing them to protect them against future defaulting and hedging them to protect them. Again, borrowing abroad is increasing the other's position in the global world but weaken yourself. So, banning all global loans, etc.

International laws regarding international credit and debt.

iv. We must establish new courts that deal with global debt in the transitional phases before ultimately outlawing international borrowing. Institutions like the IMF are acting only to perpetuate the imbalances and inequalities and they are dead to us. We need solutions and honesty it's not working. They are like loan sharks even though they don't demand the money back their subsidiaries might impose sanctions and other unfavorable economic attributes slowing growth and development. I will look at the IMF below.

National sovereign must mean just that.

v. What I think is a current problem is the lack of education in most developing leaders about money management and the best way out of this vicious circle. They say knowledge is power. My stance is to view everyone as your enemy, and you can never gain anything from them as they are your competitors so how can they have your interest at heart. The best way is to tackle all your problems yourself. Why if you are a sovereign nation rely on another country to tell you how to run your sovereign country? Why borrow from them when you can simply print and boost your people in the process.

Selfish of governments.

vi. The idea lies behind the fact that most governments think it's being reduced in value if they are there to serve the people and be indebted to them forever. But this must be the sole existence of any government because without the people the government wouldn't exist. Who will they serve? So why not do whatever it takes to increase the value of your own? Why borrow and increase risks of attack in case you default when you can exercise your rights and simply print.

vii. Fear not about the debt. This is the way things are intended to be as the debt as I explained above will simply be written off to cancel out the indebtedness between you and the government. This is the natural way. The only way to grow. All other methods I can tell you that they are just fantasies to keep a few jobs for nothing. You are sovereign why not print?

Section XVIIIg

Role of our laws in global empowerment and economic development.

i. Our laws and policies are drafted in such a way that if you give the people the focus, they need everything will follow. Go out of your way. Think outside the box and do whatever it takes to make your people happy. You can please the whole people globally but if you ignore the local people, you won't last in power. Look at the Middle East and Africa. These nations ignore the simple common rules. You are indebted to the people and everything else follows.

ii. Our laws set the record straight. Most adopt austerity measures to boost the economy but how can cuts solve problems. It's like a bodybuilder starving himself when he what's growing big. Supply is the only answer relying on the fact that the multiplier effect or trickling down effect will provide a cushion to any crunches or crisis. Governments can simply write off the debt. They can simply say money is missing with no effect whatsoever apart from the only fact that the balance sheet won't balance which can be balanced by ghost figures and still the President or Prime Minister remains in power. But it's a different situation when the people are hungry, out of jobs, with cuts everywhere with other nations calling for your head.

www.ingramcontent.com/pod-product-compliance
Lightning Source LLC
Chambersburg PA
CBHW021413210526
45463CB00001B/353